A Poetic Plunge

With
Natalie Gilmore

A HUGE Thank You! ... to those who donated to make this project possible. I am forever grateful for your support.

[Benjamin Krause] [Sienna Lyons]

[Sasha Bazhenova] [Susie Hayasaka]

[Franco & Hannah Firpo] [Annette L.]

[Robert Izzard] [Brittany Markle] [Mike Faello]

[Sohei Sugihara] [Kayla Curto] [Mandy Heflin]

[Nick Anthony] [Marc] [Liliyana S.]

[Grace Derocha] [Nicole Russo- Henderson]

[Tamara Diles Lissandrello] [Sarah Siebert]

[Aj Harpold] [Alex Schoendorf] [Aki]

[Lindsay Richardson] [KiLeigh Williams]

[Emma Werler] [Kate Schofield] [Diane Lee]

[Lindsey White] [Kim Seipel] [Flor Banchio]

[Arthur & Mathilde] [Tetiana Kocherhan]

[August Mailand] [Adam St. John]

[Mikka Wild] [JP Deapera]

Book Cover by: Anika Macias

INTRODUCTION

I promise I'll keep this short.
(Long book intros make me antsy.)
I'm a kid at heart with an independent hardshell exterior. I'm also an extremely sensitive and emotional being. My childhood was for the most part what a privileged human would call "normal." I did the public-school thing and enjoyed some after school hobbies. Dancing became my favorite hobby around age 6. The joy it brought me, and the exhilaration I got from performing has kept me dancing all the way to this very day.

After high school things got a little less "normal." I ventured away from my hometown to pursue some far-out dreams that sometimes even I didn't think were possible. Since then, I've been blessed to have experienced some amazing things. I often feel I've won a different type of life lottery. I feel my story has unfolded in the way that it has for me to be able to share it. Share the magic of occasionally floating calmly in smooth waters, or diving deep to avoid the wild waves life brings.

I think I was 13 or 14 when we first studied poems in my literature classes in school. I was fascinated by the magic that could be captured in both short and long form poems. I loved that some of them had no clear structure at all. They often felt like scattered words, but when you looked closely there was a window into another world right there before your eyes.

Here's your chance to plunge into my world a bit. This book is divided into two parts. You can read The NOW before the THEN, or maybe you want to do the opposite and start from the early years of my story and work your way into where I am now. Feel free to skip around randomly if that's more your style.

Each poem is followed by a P.S. (Plunge Story) which is a more person-to-person reflection of what I felt or feel about each poem. It has taken me close to 5 years to write this book. Nevertheless, every poem plays a role in my story, and holds a special place in my heart.

Here in these pages, I will take you with me into an ocean of memories. Floating through joyful waters of eminent times, together with deep dives into the downhearted ones too.

Please enjoy... A Poetic Plunge with Natalie Gilmore.

The NOW

Almost 3 years ago, I chose to make a crazy shift in my life. I chose to pack up my life in LA, and move across the world to Berlin, Germany to live with my at the time fiancé, now husband. After the pandemic, I felt ready to start a new adventure. I felt in my heart that it was time for a big change.

Little did I know, it would be one of the most challenging and life altering changes of my life thus far. Isolated from my community as well as everything that was familiar, I dove deep into a place of solitude and quickly became aware of all the parts of me that I had not yet faced.

I was a new Nat, in a new place, searching for some familiarity to hold on to. I didn't find much of that at the start. Learning German, while starting fresh in a similar but different industry, had its pros and cons alike. I can't say that I'm fully settled in this new life, but I can say that I'm proud of the things I've overcome and discovered in the process.

I'm slowly sifting through the conditioned beliefs that were once set values in my life. I am forging a new path with new ideals lighting the way.

Here forward is a collection of poems written in those adaptive times. They reflect many of the emotions that have flowed in and through me during this massive change. I am still learning the new Nat and uncovering all the new adventures that are meant for her here. I am slowly feeling a new fire light inside of me that is burning new energy into everything that I do.

Uprooted

Elusively lucid in a forest of space.
Not exactly sure where to turn,
not familiar with home base.
Anxious in adaptation.
Adjusting adamantly.
Cautious at every turn,
mind and heart feeling the burn.
I thought the shifts would be smoother.
Calm like a lake,
in the wake of the morning dew.
But the water rushes in and out with different force daily.
Surfing, sailing or scuba diving,
I'll find a way maybe.

P.S. - Uprooted

My partner and I dated long-distance for about 2 years. We had for a while spoken about the possibility of me moving to Berlin to start a life together. He is a dedicated father to two amazing children, and I knew that I would never want him to move far away from them.

During and after the pandemic, a lot of things had changed within the dance industry. So many jobs were restricted, or simply not happening. The entertainment world took a screeching halt, and a couple of the dance studios where I would train and teach at were forced to close their doors. Although it was very sad, it also allowed me to really think about my place in LA, and how I wanted to continue forward. I had lived in LA for 16 years at this time and had accomplished so much of what I first set out to do. During those work focused years, I often longed to build my personal life too. Focusing so deeply on the work and achievements, I think I didn't really give my personal life a fair chance.

And now here was that chance. The chance to work on another important aspect of my life, and I was ready to give it a fair shot. So, I packed up my whole life, and moved to Berlin in August of 2021.

Re-planted

I've been re-planted in new soil.
New roots wiggling in,
as I sift through the weeds of my past on the way down.
Nutrients of all kinds nurture these new veins,
as I continue to connect with this new place.
Fertilizing the growth of a new seed planted.
Absorbing the surrounding sunlight,
as I photosynthesize into developed expansion.
Shooting my way through the moss.
I sprout.
Then bud.
Then bloom.
Maybe this time,
a tree with leaves that come and go with each season.
Or a flower whose nectar nourishes the bees
to progress the ecosystem.
All of which have their time,
and then begin new again.
That's where I stand.
Anew with a new view.
Ready for all that's to come.

P.S. - Re-planted

This one I wrote about how it felt to be uprooted from my LA life and re-planted into my new Berlin life. It felt like I was sifting through the soil but couldn't quite see how it would all bloom. That feeling still comes in waves. Everything is different. I mean everything. My environment, the food, the language, the culture, the weather, my work and my home. Sheesh!

Sometimes I'm still not sure how I'm doing it. But at that time, deep inside, there was also an excitement. Something that was telling me this was the perfect time for me to get a fresh start. To bloom where I was in whatever way that I could at that time. Three years later, I'm still ironing out the details. I have times where it gets hard mentally, and times where I'm so thankful for the opportunity to start fresh with the support system that I have. I am a constantly budding plant that is feeling her way through the new soil every day.

I fell

I fell quickly and unexpectedly,
to a place I didn't know yet.
I fell in slow motion.
A fall
that called me
to crawl back tall,
into a newer version of me.
A bit shook, confused, off-balance and scraped up.
But like leaves falling in fall,
I want to float down with patience,
through this season of transformation.

P.S. - I fell

I wrote this short poem after I actually fell off my bike one day. I was just running a few simple errands close by, and on my way home I caught the edge of the curb at the wrong angle. I let go of the bike to not crush my legs with it, and in that very (what felt like slow-motion moment,) I caught myself by sliding against the pavement with my palms and kneecaps.
Ouch!

Thankfully, I wasn't moving too fast, and I was able to ride the rest of the way home with just a few scrapes and bruises. It had been so long since I had physically fallen. The fall had triggered so many thoughts in me. It reminded me of how I often felt in this new place. Sometimes slowly falling while feeling a bit out of control. Not able to make the same kind of living that I had made in LA. Not being able to always communicate when I was out and about. Not being able to know where this road would take me or if it was simply going to take me down.

Water Spills

Water spills.
My heart deeply fills.
Reminded of how far I've come,
and inspired by all that I've yet to become.
Moving more precisely.
Making stops and turns decisively.
Way more aware of the things that feel like ease.
Inviting a lot more of that in please.
I am already breaking the cycles.
Excited to bring forth mic fulls.
Grateful for these fresh eyes.
Only for magic will they compromise.

P.S. - Water Spills

I spilled a large glass of water on this day. Where I would normally get really frustrated, I felt a sense of perspective take over me.

My subconscious then said to me, "Forget about the water Nat, look at how far you've come." I'm not sure why that statement came at that moment, but it did, and I grinned big as I cleaned up the silly spill. It was a moment where I gave myself grace and remembered that I was doing things that some could never imagine doing in their lives. Remembering that I had accomplished so much already at this point, and I felt proud.

Really proud.

Not sure how the spilled water triggered all of that but I'm thankful it did.

Friendships Fade

Friendships fade,
in elaborate ways.
It stings pretty sharp,
to not know exactly why.
You will miss them.
But know it might be time
to let them go.
Always remember the good times,
but don't dwell too long,
'Cuz time flies.
Sometimes they visit me in my dreams.
Flashes of the friendship gleam.
I wouldn't trade the time we had,
a lot of it kept me really glad.
Making new friends isn't always easy.
The older I get the greater that feeling.
Grateful for the ones that haven't faded.
They are the reason I am a little less jaded.

P.S. - Friendships Fade

During and post pandemic a lot of people also relocated either back to their hometowns, or somewhere completely new. Some of the friendships that I had for a large portion of my life had faded out. Those friendships all felt so influential to my life. They were people who had been with me through some tough times, as well as some incredibly euphoric ones. Watching them fade out was hard. It hurt a lot. I stopped hearing from them, and I understood why.

Sometimes understanding it makes it even harder. You see it. You get it. But you aren't quite ready to let go. But yes, life will show us when it's time to let go, even if we don't want to. The resistance to it is what causes the suffering within us. I allowed myself to mourn the changes, but I also reflected on all the memories we had made that will be with me forever. If you're one of those friends that faded away, just know that I understand, and will forever cherish the memories we made.

Thank You for being in my life for the time that you were. You really helped me through a lot.

Adjustments

Adjustments falling in line.
New journeys divine.
Missing only the comforts that once were.
Finding new ones to incur.
A great escape from the norm that once was.
Inspired to see what the universe does.
Appreciative of all that has been.
Excited for every new win.
Expression has been minimal.
Feelings bottled up invincible.
Navigating new waters in a new boat.
Learning to keep my heart afloat.
Becoming more of what I've always been.
Each day allowing a little more in.
I am me and only me.
Adjusting the vision with new clarity.

P.S. - Adjustments

When I wrote this it really felt like every day I was finding small adjustments. Like when you crack your knuckles and can feel that little realignment that just needed to be. Parts of my life were coming together, and others were falling apart. I was adjusting accordingly as best I could. I felt grateful to start fresh but was also looking and feeling for how exactly I wanted to do that. Little by little, I see the adjustments smoothing out. I am excited for more adjustments and more smoothing out.

I guess in life the adjusting and smoothing process is the ebb and flow of it all. Change is constant, even if you stay in one place forever. Learning to smoothly move through the change has been my greatest practice as well as my greatest internal battle.

Change

Change is a range of emotion.
A transformation potion.
Ever pivoting angles, you once thought you knew well,
connecting your confusion and delusion into dwell.
Often an internal hell.
A space you don't want to sit down in.
A space that feels uncomfortable.
But the space you need to move into a new comfort.
Backwards as it may feel,
those fearful layers we need to peel.
Stop worrying about what others may be thinking,
and experience deeply everything between blinking.
Zoom in on the moments you don't know
which way to go.
Breathe deep, and slowly connect each row.
Each row holds a power.
Let them bloom like flowers.
Slowly build a dream tower.
Tackle it with glower.
Let the change be your guide,
it is a huge part of the ride.
Once we can accept it in stride,
heart and mind less often divide.

P.S. - Change

I say it in this poem "Let the change be your guide." This part is essential, especially when the change is not so comfortable. I've never been so good with change when it's forced, but I'm also not afraid to take a leap into the unknown. Those seem to counteract each other, but it's the truth. Sometimes I may not be so prepared for what's to come, but who is? As humans we crave the familiar.

The things and people that bring us comfort. But the funny thing is, one of the biggest constants in life is change. Always shifting and lifting us into new versions of ourselves. There is not one magic way to handle it, especially when the change may be sudden or extra uncomfortable. But these shifts whether big or small are there for a reason. A reason we may not know yet.

I guess what I've learned is the only way out is through. We must feel the feelings, and work on shifting the ones that we can. Understanding and trusting that maybe what we had is no longer with us for a reason. Trusting that maybe, just maybe, there is something grander on the horizon.

After making a huge change in my life, uprooting from the home I knew for 16 years, and building a new life from scratch in a different country, the only thing I've really been able to cling to is taking things one day at a time.

I try to remember that in each new day we can start new, both in our actions and in our mindset alike. The waves of life will come and go. Sometimes you'll float in calm waters and other times you'll need a surfboard to get you back to shore. In both cases we are in control of how we feel and think in the process of it. That's also where we find our greatest inner peace.

My Roots

I can tell my roots are dry,
not currently energized or spry.
Dehydrated from recent adventures.
So many possible potentials.
Standing tall but feeling weak.
My creative branches have started to creak.
The leaves have fallen,
come back,
and will fall again soon.
I'm hoping to feel revived around June.
Or maybe even better by noon.
I'm ready to swoon,
and create.
Not hesitate to embrace the different states.
Each one has its place in the grandest of ways.
I'm hoping water is on the way.
In the wind, I've started to sway.
To accept the fact that I'm not at my strongest,
but ready to persevere for the longest.

P.S. - My Roots

I've always admired that trees can look so still and bare, and yet be so alive in their roots. Even when their leaves fall, they are at their strongest. They weather the seasons with perseverance. They gather their strength from mother nature. They provide oxygen, our life force.

I'm grateful for trees. Here personifying myself as a tree was in connection with how I was feeling when I wrote this poem.

Roots dry.
Preparing for seasons to come.
Swaying in the winds of change.
Creatively creaking from all the swaying.
Persevering through the weather of it all.
Remaining tall and appearing strong
even when I may not feel like it.

Butterfly

I feel a return to my love for me
coming slowly.
All that has changed within me,
is reflected radiance.
New expressions.
Self-reflection.
Embodied throughout.
Butterfly from the cocoon.
She rises with fresh wings,
expanding into the ether.
Fluttering through a new space,
with a fresh sky scrolling by.
A new perspective on how she wants to present herself.
Taking with her, small parts of her past self.
But ultimately landing on new ground.
There's so much to be found.
The hibernation she endured was her greatest blessing.
It now launches her forward with new musings.
Expressed elegance,
and newfound love for a revived appearance.
Holding on tightly to the journey she has so far
experienced.
Knowing it's the journey that got her here.
Adding details along the way throughout the years.
She now flies proud in her newest shape,
awaiting patiently her next big break.

P.S. - Butterfly

The evolution and birth of a butterfly is one of the most fascinating things to me. From a fuzzy caterpillar into a boundless butterfly. A magical metamorphosis.

During big change we humans are in a "cocoon" of sorts, just before a re-birth into a "new form." The dark spaces that often feel like there's no way out. A constant reminder that we all have our own timing. Furthermore, an inspiration of that transformation ushering us into a space more open where we are free to fly high.

In the last few years, a lot of changes have come about in my life. Plenty of hibernation and self-reflection has been the result. There is a feeling that I know things are changing for the next best thing. A feeling that I am just about to emerge from my dark cocoon into a new and revitalized chapter. A feeling of being ready to fly high above all that has tried to take me down along the way.

I wrote this poem when I truly felt that feeling within me. It had been a long time since I had experienced such darkness. Let's say, it was also a very new kind of darkness. Real grown-up type of darkness is the only way I feel I can describe it. New chapters flourishing constantly, but this time so much more at stake. To become a partner, and a stepmom, while reimagining my career all at once. I was just about to fly into one of the greatest most complex chapters of my life, and I could feel it.

Whether you are in the cocoon, or have the butterflies rising within you, remember that everything comes in cycles. Nature is constantly reminding us of that. Try to enjoy where you are here in the moment and prepare yourself for the next big thing that may be just around the corner.

Out of practice

I've been wanting to write more.
Craving pen to paper but feeling pressure.
What if it's not good enough?
What if the words don't spill out of my head
like sweet caramel?
"You're out of practice" I tell myself.
"You don't know what you're doing anymore."
Who is this person that tells me who I am,
and what I know?
It's not really me.
The me I know doesn't always have all her shit together.
But the me I know believes in that shit,
even when it's not always together.
Finding peace amongst the pieces.
What is each piece showing me?
Right now, I find lack of consistency
to be the main source of trouble.
But maybe no trouble at all,
as I'm craving the wordplay double.
Loosing things and finding them again,
reminds us of the beauty we feel for a win within.

P.S. - Out of practice

When I started writing this book, it was simply to write. It was about expressing the feelings and thoughts within me. It was also about logging the timeline of the events that would take place, and how they made me feel in those moments. As soon as I got more serious about my writing, the inner critic began to play its awful role inside my head. Telling me all the reasons why it wouldn't be good enough or why I wouldn't be able to do it right, or at all.

The same thing happened as soon as I chose to make dance my career. The comparison flooded me and sometimes still does. The life of an artist is very free at times, but that same freedom can give your head the space to make up stories about how you will do it, or not.

This poem is a tribute to that, and a reminder that we can never have it all figured out. We can never have all our shit together, and that we must also celebrate that. Trusting ourselves that things are going to unfold just as they are supposed to. The trusting part has been the hardest for me. At times, I just want the answers.

Even more I crave the answer of which direction to take next. Sometimes that means taking a step back to remember why I started in the first place. Often the direction will reveal itself without you trying too hard. One of the greatest gifts I gave myself was learning how to quiet that voice in my head. I'm never able to silence it completely, but I am much more aware and in control of it now.

*Note to you and myself: Believe in your damn self and do everything you can to stay consistent and persistent in the things you find important.

I'm not

I'm not who I was.
I'm not yet who I will be.

But in the in-between comes a re-flourished me.
The clouds change form as I watch them overhead.
They don't hurry,
but expand instead.
This is how I see the versions of me.
Sometimes dense and full of emotional waters.
Often wisping delicately into the changing winds.

I'm not who I was.
I'm not yet who I will be.

But I'll let the wind carry,
and shape the greatest me.

P.S. - I'm not

I wrote this one while sitting on a beach in the north of Italy. My partner and I were on a short vacation, and he was in the water somewhere. I had looked up at the clouds and took a huge deep breath. The feeling of not being who I used to be, overwhelmed me. But then, the feeling of not yet being who I will be was exciting.

Juggling all the beautiful possibilities of who that new Nat is going to be brought a huge smile to my face. The idea that I would let the winds of change shape me just like the clouds was relieving.

It felt like a surrender. A release of pressure. Pressure I was putting on myself but that wasn't serving me anyway. A pressure that would lead me to worry was the last thing I needed. Releasing that pressure into the wind with another big sigh, I looked up at the clouds again and smiled. I pictured myself up there dancing with them into my next big chapter.

Pen to Page

There's a lot I can say about releasing pen to page.
It lets me out of my hearts cage to express some rage,
and in the same sentence sage the inner gears
that keep this machine working.
It cleanses the space where my heart sits,
and opens a place deep in my soul's pits.
The pen glides gently along the thin lines,
providing the right amount of ink to all my rhymes.
Inviting me to keep pouring out what I feel.
Adoring every moment, allowing me to heal.
Each day we connect differently.
Sometimes for business,
or others for therapy.
But steady always there for me.
Open to peeling new layers on every new page.
With the pen pressed to it,
every page becomes a stage.

P.S. - Pen to Page

I started journaling before I knew how good it was for
me. I didn't learn until much later that journaling was being
recommended by therapists to sort and acknowledge your
thoughts and emotions. It was being recommended to relieve
stress, encourage awareness and enhance creativity.

These are just a few of the amazing benefits.
I can say writing creates all of those for me and more.
You can absolutely journal on your phone or computer; how-
ever, I am a lover of the feeling of pen to paper.

This poem is simply about the feelings writing brings me
and the relationship I have with it.

Souls Tattoo

Putting things off,
just simply out of fear.
Mainly fear of assuming how they'll turn out.
Putting things in a corner of mind that hasn't seen light
for weeks.
Churning it like butter,
the consistency only gets thicker.
Shying away from the things that make me feel whole.
I often feel like just crawling into a hole.
It's not that I don't believe in the things that I make,
but will others believe in it enough to intake?
To intake the depths of the place it all came from.
Digging deep in my heart but my lungs simply numb.
It makes it hard to breathe.
To feel.
To leap.
To see.
See who I truly am,
and how I want to show it.
Or do I rather show the places where I've been hit?
Maybe showing the scars that make up my soul's tattoo,
will be the very words that carry mine and other hearts
through.

P.S. - Souls Tattoo

I've often felt like I don't really fit in. Maybe, it's just that I haven't found exactly where I do. Or maybe I was never meant to.

Being an artist is hard.

Finding an audience that resonates with your work can be a slow process. In the time in between we toss around thoughts of not doing or being enough. Fear of no one listening. Fear of judgement from those who may not understand. Pressure pressing on us to make more and be more.

But if there's one thing I know now, it is that art is where pain and suffering are celebrated. Where people can share their pain unfiltered and hear a round of applause. It's the place where people in pain go to feel connected to something bigger than them.

Through our pain and art, we can all connect. But it takes that artist sharing their pain to create the space for others to do so. I've felt all the artist feelings and feel now is my time to share my story to possibly give that space to others.

If you dare

I'm trying to let more things annoy me less.
Giving myself more emotional rest.
Often adjusting to find that best feeling place.
A journey into each space, no need to race.
One thing at a time, that's what can be held in your mind.
You are so much more than the things that you do.
Please find something that fills you too.
Fills you with feeling feeling-type things.
Ones that make your heart ring, and your soul sing.
You are the whole choir.
Creating the harmonies that you desire.
You can generate the vibrato when things feel staccato.
You are the conductor of your own symphony.
Don't be afraid to approach it differently.
Then enjoy the joy when you find moments of peace.
Take in the waves, while relaxing on the beach.
Or ride the waves on a self-love surfboard,
to calmer waters both forward and toward.
Braving life's waters just to get there.
Rewarded with care if you dare to show up bare.

P.S. - If you dare

This one came to me while taking a step back from one thing and finding the joy and excitement from another. Remembering that finding joy in each of our days must be a priority. We need joy. That feeling when we can truly enjoy something, unlocks a part of our heart that opens other worlds of possibility.

At times my dance students have expressed to me the burnout that comes from never taking a break from that one thing. I always advise them to find something else that brings them joy and do that for a while.

Mine is arts and crafts. Making things by hand that I can be proud of. When I'm doing those types of activities, I go into a similar meditative, joyful, flow state like the one I fall into when I'm dancing. I have very often felt like "I can't take a break." Feeling like if I don't stay consistent, then I'll lose the momentum and everything that I've been working up to will somehow be lost. Yes, it's true that you may lose some momentum in that area, but what if you gain momentum in another. You may be pleasantly surprised at what you find along the way. It is also not likely that you will lose everything you learned. Some things may feel farther away, but you can always pick up where you left off and see where it takes you.

The point is when you open to the joy of other things, you are simply opening to joy, which is something that can often help make things lighter, brighter and smoother.

Home

Home has always been within,
but often outside forces make us feel we can't win.
So, then we pin this feeling to ourselves.
We allow our head, and hearts to swell.
We get consumed by what we cannot do,
and forget that we cannot do it
a part.
Apart from others, but more importantly ourselves.
We separate from our inner home,
and convince ourselves the outside world is the norm.
We compare and relate,
sometimes confused thoughts turn to hate.
We continue outside until it gets dark and cold.
We convince ourselves of the terrible fold.
But the fold in our heart
is also a guide back to our art.
It's where the turning point shines in gold.
Remember to check in with your own,
and allow yourself to return back home.

P.S. - Home

Finding my home within has been both a blessing and a struggle. At times, I've felt far away from myself, floating aimlessly through the world. Others I've felt far away from the outside world, but at the same time so connected to myself.

I believe there is benefit in both feelings. Sometimes floating aimlessly leads you to a place that you didn't know you needed or wanted to find. And sometimes disconnecting from the outside world leads you right to the place within that you need to sit with to choose your next move.

I personally feel more at ease when I can connect to my inner world. For me, the best way to do that is through meditation. I began learning and practicing meditation about 10 years ago. I have a dear friend who at the time was completing her yoga teacher training hours at the dance studio I worked at, and she introduced me to both yoga and meditation.

At first, my sessions were short and fidgety. I couldn't quite "drop in" to that serene space that so many spoke of. I didn't know how to allow my thoughts to just be. To see the thoughts for what they were. Just thoughts.

Eventually coming to realize that not every thought had to be a reality. Acknowledging that a lot of my thoughts were influenced by my upbringing, and the mentalities of those around me during that time. Letting go of a lot of those constructs allowed me to drop into that serene space in my heart.

When I am in that space, what is going on around and outside of me can still be important but impacts me differently. I let myself be with myself, and the rest can wait.

Daily Business

The sun slides in
through the windows screen.
A soft silence takes me
to a land of daydream.
Loose dust dances on the sun rays,
moving together as if they were on stage.
My colorful sweater hugs me real close.
A deep belly breath fills me the most.
I love this feeling of simple stillness.
I will manifest it into my daily business.

P.S. - Daily Business

This poem was written in a moment of reflection as I sat at my desk at home. I stopped to take a deep breath as the sun was creeping in through the window. It was a moment where everything felt in slow motion. I saw the dust particles as I had many times before, but this time I watched them long enough to see them dancing. Floating freely while enjoying some sunshine. While observing my senses, I wrote about the ones that stood out the most. This is my written version of what mindfulness feels like.

You can do this at anytime and anywhere that you may be. It doesn't have to be a long moment, but simply a mindful one to observe and enjoy the little things right in front of you.

The little things that sometimes feel really big.
I try to make this a part of my daily business. It brings me back to a centered feeling almost every time. Even if just for one minute, I am fully with myself, and the moment before me. I feel more connected to the world and my life as I'm experiencing it right then and there.

Some days it's easier than others.
Some days I forget.
I guess that's part of being human.

There will always be days where we are more present and connected than others, but I truly believe it's a practice. Like with anything, the more often we do it, the better at it we'll get.

Floating

My getaway boat to a place of precise peace.
Astronauts exploring the universe's every crease.
A leaf that leaves a tree to have a dance with the air.
Apples bounce buoyantly with endless giggles to share.
Balloons instantly celebrate another year has passed.
Vanilla ice cream floats to the top of a foamy glass.
Ice plunking down into your favorite summer drink.
Birds gliding high soaring splendidly in sync.
A bottle rises sending a message of love into motion.
Thought bubbles that float
consistently in my minds ocean.
Sometimes they spark stars in the dark parts of my mind,
or flames that flicker freely joining my passions divine.
And I, with ears underwater, drown out the outside noise.
On my back, arms out, toes high, I surrender with poise.
Deep breaths echo in my head,
while the air fills my chest,
like a built-in life vest.
The air creates a forcefield.
The water pressure presses me,
pushing all my loose parts back to feel.
Allowing the current to currently move me.
In this moment,
just float,
just be.

P.S. - Floating

I'm fascinated by the idea and feeling of floating. It reminds me of being a kid.

Floating in a pool of water.
Balloons soaring gently in the wind.
Bobbing for apples with grand giggles.
I mean c'mon … astronauts walking on the moon with no gravity.

The idea of weightlessness also brings me a sense of ease. A feeling that one can relax even if in a small way for just a short time.

This poem was inspired by all the things I could think of that float, and the picture they paint when they do.

I also turned this one into a spoken word piece with some basic choreography. I hope it made you smile, and I am excited to perform it live for you all someday.

Shooting Star

I saw a shooting star tonight.
It quickly trailed off into the same night.
I'm sure into another galaxy in the skies,
like the one I visit when I close my eyes.
A wish made for a life I know is coming.
I imagine my nurturing space dawning.
The future castle where the king and queen
come home to rest.
Where the kids play freely, safe from the worlds arrest.

P.S. - Shooting Star

I did see a shooting star just before I wrote this.
And I did wish for a world that I knew was coming. I refuse to give into the idea that there is more hate than love in the world. I feel that's what the media often feeds us, and so we often believe that to be the only truth.

But I believe in a different world.
I believe in the one where we help each other and build each other up before tearing each other down. This poem depicts a very cliché expression of what an ideal home or world could look like. I use it as a metaphor to the wish I have that the lovers of this world will turn up the volume. Not only at home but in the world. That's how we shift the narrative amongst ourselves and quiet what the media says in our heads. Living in a way that we all support each other, and love on one another as neighbors.

I believe in that, and if I ever see another shooting star I'll wish for that exact same thing.

For the dreamers

Here's to the ones who dream,
foolish as they may seem.
Creatives who strive to constantly beam,
but inside sometimes they scream.
Needing to let off steam.
Their goals they deem,
as they burst at the seam.
Pressure filling their blood stream.
Expectations extreme.
Looking for a support team.
Ever shifting themes.
Time to plot a new scheme to dream.

P.S. - For the dreamers

This poem was written for those artists who feel these things and is also a tribute to the first feature film I had the privilege of working on as a dancer. LaLa Land is yes, a love story, but also an artist's story. So, I started the poem with a line from my favorite song on the soundtrack.

During the pandemic I started a program called GUID-ANCE with Nat. The program was originally meant to be an in-person program. I had everything set up, and the week before it was to begin, I got the call that all the studios were closing due to this thing that we were hearing about on the news but didn't know much about.

I was sad that I wouldn't be able to carry out this idea how I had envisioned it. So as many did during these times, I adjusted and moved everything online. It allowed so many other artists from all over the world to join. I didn't know it at the time, but it was truly a blessing in disguise. I didn't know that I would be so deeply moved by the stories of these artists. Stories not only about themselves and their goals, but of their fears and mental roadblocks that met them along the way.

The first sessions were more about movement refinement. But after having my 1-on-1 calls with them, I realized that their greatest blocks were more mental than physical. They were overwhelmed by their inner critics, and compared so much of what they did with that of others. That's when I realized a bigger part of my purpose. I already knew I enjoyed teaching dance, but I saw something in those students that I remembered battling myself as a young aspiring dancer. I knew in those next few sessions that I wanted to dive deeper into helping artists nurture their mental health throughout their artistic journey.

Soul Sisters

You see me for who I am,
and don't judge me for any reactions.
Instead, when I react you soften,
and dig into the places that are hurting.
You tell me your stories of how you can relate,
and we always close out with belly laughs to escape.
You are someone who is just as ambitious
and driven as I am,
and that pushes me farther.
It reminds me how beautiful it feels to make your own,
and travel the road least followed.
We are similar,
but so different.
The yin to my yang.
Thank You.
I really couldn't ask for a better girl gang.

P.S. - Soul Sisters

This one is dedicated to any woman who has shown up for me in the way I describe in this poem. There haven't been many, but I thought of every one of you when I was writing it.

There is something so special about finding your tribe of women. Connecting with women who support you, as well as telling you the truth even when it hurts. Women who motivate you to work harder and show up in their lives authentically. Women who celebrate you in both little and big ways.

I vow to do my best to always be this person for you all, and I want to celebrate all the little and big wins with you until we're old and grey.

I love you all so much.
Thank You Eternally.

Dear little Nat

Dear little Nat,

You have no idea how incredibly capable you are.
How much your hard work will pay off, and how much
light you will bring into this world.
You don't know it yet, but you have some abandonment
trauma, and this will trigger you to seek love from people
who can't give it back to you.
They won't be able to pour back the amounts of love and
loyalty you gift them.
And that's ok, because in the process of it all...
you will learn.
You will learn to heal yourself from within,
and in that process stumble gracefully
upon a love you've always dreamed of.
Keep believing.
Stay hopeful.
Stay happy.
I love you.
You're doing a great job.

- Big Nat

P.S. - Dear little Nat

I wrote this as an exercise from a writing workshop I took. At first, I felt frustrated that it was short. I wanted it to be more lengthy and profound. Somehow, I had an expectation of what my little Nat needed to hear that day.

On that same day, I sat back staring at what I wrote, and realized that it was the first time I had written some of those things down. I had talked through most of them in my head before, but I had never seen them with my eyes. Seeing them with my eyes that day did something to me.

My eyes welled up in tears, and I realized that exercise was part of the healing I needed to do in that moment. It wasn't about the length of the poem, and it wasn't about the vocabulary I used. It was about those few lines that I was aware of and no longer afraid to write down.

I think I had never written them down because that would make them all too real in some way. But on that day, they were real, and I accepted them as my truth. I wanted to tell my little Nat that everything was going to be ok.

I think I told Big Nat the same thing that day.

This Time

This time is a place.
Can time even be a place?
Can we place time where we want it?
Can we hold time for a special place?
There's a time for every place,
and a place for every time.
And when place and time collide,
we feel memories.
Feelings of what that time meant to us,
and how that place felt for us.
Looking back on old places,
excited for new and bright spaces.
Are spaces like places?
I guess,
depending on different cases.
In this case, there's no time to waste.
Grab your seconds by the hand,
and cherish the place in plan.
Don't let time stop you.
Follow what feels true,
and allow yourself,
and the world to be renewed.

P.S. - This Time

Oh Time! Time is often so confusing. Time is a construct that man made to keep track of the days. It often doesn't feel real to me.

Yes, time passes of course, but the question I ask myself is... is it really passing or simply cycling? I have so many questions about time. I won't put them all here.

Sometimes I let time rule me, and the way I do things. Schedules. Deadlines. "I'm getting older." Life is too short.

Other times I want to let go of time completely. I want to sleep when I'm sleepy. Work when I'm inspired. Let things happen when they are meant to happen.

How do you feel about time?

New Lingo

Feeling into foreign phrases.
Syllables sizzle,
while confidence raises.
Learning wordage and sayings.
Meanings and metaphors slaying.
Diving into descriptions.
Delicate definitions.
Striving for elegant enunciation,
while practicing perfecting quotation.
Thoughts slowly seep into utterances.
Every day a few more sentences.
Vivacious verses,
and emphatic euphemisms.
Thirty minutes daily I've promised myself,
hoping the fluency develops itself.

P.S. - New Lingo

Have you ever tried to learn a new language in your late thirties? HA! It's really hard. Let's say, especially German.

I've always been in awe of how many languages exist, and shocked at how each one of them can sound so different. So, after moving to Germany, I decided that I wanted to start learning German. Being already bilingual made me think that I would be alright. Woo Wee!!! I had no idea what I was getting myself into.

The grammar is the hardest part. Also, pronouncing some of the words with 25 letters often feels like climbing Mt. Everest with my mouth. After two and a half years, I have to say it's getting more fun. I'm understanding much more and I'm getting a little braver to speak it. I have dreamt that I'm fluent, and I know I'll make that dream a reality someday. In the meantime, wish me luck.

Bonus Mom

From one day to the next,
my whole life changed.
My priorities would soon re-organize and re-arrange.
Two new souls I didn't know I'd meet.
Learning them both has been a grandiose feat.
Life became more about what's for dinner,
or who could in a race be the winner.
Each at their own stage,
they grow in tremendous ways.
I only want what's best for them.
From me, I hope some inspiration stems.
I can never get it all right.
But through the years, I focus on their light.
Expanding in ways unknown,
hoping to give them the greatest second home.

P.S. - Bonus Mom

I'll start by saying that bonus mom-ing is so hard. But I will also say that I have found some amazing resources and support out there to better understand the role, and some of the challenges that come with it. I will also say that I have been very blessed to be accepted and loved on by my two bonus kiddos in the process.

I care about them very much and am excited to watch them grow into their own selves. Now that some of the initial noise and shock has settled, I am able to see them as two humans just developing and finding their way on their own path. I won't always be able to help them, but I can do my best to be there for and support them through it.

I've always had a very motherly nature. Some things feel natural, and others feel like I'm upside down in my own world. I hope they both will always know that they can come to me for anything.

If you're a stepmom out there and have any amazing books or resources, please share them with me. This is just the beginning of what I know will be a lifelong ride.

Away Message

Stepping away from all that I knew.
Wishing to grow,
and expand anew.
It's hard being away from those I love.
Sometimes I just need a really big hug.
I've sailed away from the familiar before,
this time becoming familiar with more.
More of what I want,
and who I want to be.
Sinking far away
from what used to be me.

P.S. - Away Message

If there was still AOL instant messenger, this would have been my away message for the last two years.

(And if you don't know what that is just think status on WhatsApp or a note on your IG) :)

Balance

Tipping the scales a little in each direction daily.
Finding a bit more connection
to the things I know
I want more of.
At the forefront,
more self-love.
Expressing elaborately in calming new ways.
Extending eloquently into simpler days.
There are so many ways to create balance.
Striving daily for eternal valance.

P.S. - Balance

I feel life is always about finding a balance. Balance between the things you love to do, and those you must do. Balance between the things that make you sad, and finding more things that make you glad. Balance between work, and the things that fill up your cup.

Sometimes the scale can tip very far in one direction, and that's when we must create our own balance in all of it. One thing I've really been clinging to is the thought that we can create that balance.

We are in control.
(Most of the time.)

We only need to want to create that balance to get closer to it.

Me Tree

What used to be,
is no longer.
My true values only creep in stronger.
With reminders of how I want to be treated,
without the in-between being repeated.
Slowly turning toward the things that feel good.
Prioritizing little bits of my childhood.
Standing my ground,
and not settling for less,
usually doesn't come without stress.
I dig deeper every day,
to find what puts my heart at bay.
In the process I imagine all that could be,
growing by the minute into the tree that is me.

P.S. - Me Tree

So many things changed after I moved away from LA almost 3 years ago.

What I didn't expect was that my values would light up so bright. Things I used to find normal, were no longer acceptable. My standards in relationships both personal and professional significantly raised. I was no longer accepting any behavior that didn't feel respectful, and I was forced to see the reality that some of the friendships that I so deeply cherished faded when it got a bit more difficult to catch up.

The new reality was sometimes not so fun, but I felt the truth behind those realities. I felt another layer of who I am emerging. I now see the value in upholding the standards and values I have for myself. They bring me returned respect. They remind me that I am worthy of that returned respect.

There are some parts of my old life that I miss for sure. But this feeling of empowerment has been the greatest take away.

New Shoes

My old pair of shoes don't fit anymore.
They've been through a lot,
now beat up and worn.
My new pair of shoes feel fresh and sturdy,
supporting me through this era of thirties.
The old pair isn't bad,
but after a while
they hurt my feet.
The new ones are showing me the way
of a brand-new street.
A street that feels smooth, calming and wide.
One where I feel there's no need to hide.
I'll take them for a walk,
and enjoy their warmth.
Taking simple strides
in an inspiring direction forth.

P.S. - New Shoes

The old shoes I'm referring to in this case are my "dancing shoes." Changing shoes in real life can be so relieving, but new shoes can also be very uncomfortable. You have to break them in a bit. The idea of "changing shoes" that I've worn for so long has been daunting.

Do I want to take them off for a while? For how long? Will they feel as cozy as they once did when I put them back on? Am I ready for a new pair of shoes? They look fresh and ready for new adventures, but the question is... am I ready to go with them?

That old comfy pair of shoes are worn and tired, but they are familiar. I know how they feel on my feet. But I feel myself slowly settling into the new shoes, and the adventures they are wanting to take me on. Although very different from my previous adventures it feels great to step outside of my norm. The new shoes here being my "writer/poet shoes."

Besides the occasional emotional ups and downs, I am enjoying the new shoes. It is the first time in my life that I really felt called to try on new shoes. Dance will forever be a passion of mine, but I have seen and realized so much of that adventure. My heart is calling for things new and refreshed.

It will take a bit to break the new shoes in, but that's part of the journey, right? I'm taking it in stride and trying not to anticipate too far into the future of what will happen or how.

For a Capricorn like me that is a tough task. But I feel the shift. I feel the benefits it has already brought me in the short time that I've stayed committed. Are you in a new shoe era, or maybe perfectly cozy in the familiar shoes you're wearing?

To the clouds

I am definitely in a cloud.
Nothing feels the same somehow.
Somehow, you knew just how to love us all.
Maybe you didn't want to let us see you fall.
Superman now flying high through the clouds,
leaving strategic sparks in all of your rounds.
Eloquent elegance flowed from your baritone,
a tone that rose from deep within your soul.
A force in many fields.
Always bringing us so many feels.
Wisdom in your movement.
Musicality in your humanity.
Your hugs put me back together.
You empowered us to keep getting better.
I will miss you so very very much.
To the happy memories I will always clutch.
An icon in our hearts worthy of deep veneration.
We will honor you through our greatest creations.
And when I miss you most, to the clouds I'll glance.
To catch you smiling through your eternal dance.

P.S. - To the clouds

I lost an amazing friend in December of 2022. He was a light everywhere he went. His smile would make you smile no matter what. He gave the tightest hugs and was an incredible creative and mover. He influenced me deeply as a young dancer by always offering love and support in my journey. He was someone who saw me genuinely as an artist and vocalized his recognition often.

His passing shocked us all. It was very unexpected. This poem spilled out of me the day after I found out. I was in such a daze, but also so clear on what I wanted to say to him.

This shocking news shed a bright light on the mental health struggles that artists often face. A smile on camera or social media doesn't always look the same behind closed doors. This event, as tragic as it was also reaffirmed the part of me that wants to be a safe space for artists and their mental health throughout their journey.

This poem is for you Stephen.
I think of you often and will never forget all the things you taught me.

*If you or someone you know is struggling with mental health, please don't hesitate to ask for help. There are so many resources out there, don't be afraid to use them.

Stay in the day

I long to stay in the day
where everyone can see their worth.
See that simple newborn that they were right at birth.
Then watch themselves grow up slowly,
and savor every chapter lovingly.
Not be afraid to make mistakes,
or say what's on their mind,
inviting all the differences they find in humankind.
Feel into themselves, and the things that hurt them.
Accepting what is now and leaving the past in then.
Dancing in the beauty of being new every single day.
Hugging themselves tightly in every single way.
Remembering that we are all fighting our own battles.
Expanding, and demanding,
every day comes more compassion.
Compassion for the tiny inner child in us all.
Reaching for love and extra support when we fall.
Giving grace to those who make mistakes,
and comforting them through the highest stakes.
Allowing every kind of human to be simply humankind.
Embracing every story without ever hitting rewind.
Letting each person be who they want to be,
but most of all remembering to set yourself free.
It all begins with you, and how you feel about yourself.
The value you hold for your mind, body and soul
is your eternal wealth.
Let's stay in the day where we can all see our worth,
enjoying each other together
on this blissful, magical Earth.

P.S. - Stay in the day

I wrote this poem during the pandemic. I could feel so much darkness in the world. Not only because of the pandemic, but also because we were watching so many displays of blatant racism. The message is a bit of what some would call a dreamers wish. The message simply being that we are all humankind and practicing that kindness towards one another no matter where we come from is what I believe will heal us along with the world.

Not everyone, everywhere, or all at once, but small acts every day can create and grow that love and unity. Maybe just in your own community to start. The most important part is that kindness comes only when you can know and love yourself first. This is the part that I believe so many don't put as the priority. Working on ourselves is hard. Getting to know the many versions of ourselves is hard. But that's my dreamers wish for the world.

Compassion for one another. Kindness towards one another. We don't all have the same access and ability to get to know and love ourselves. But for those who do and can, let's spread the kindness. None of us can pour from an empty cup, so do your best to fill yours up first, and then share the wealth as much as you can.

The THEN

A collection of poems that reflect some noteworthy moments from my childhood all the way into my thirties. These are some of the most influential moments and people that I can recall.

I went on an incredible emotional journey while trying my best to capture these moments as vividly as I remember them. These are just fragments of the bigger picture that is the story of my life so far. I pay tribute to the influential characters and moments in time that played huge roles in my life. I could never include every detail, but I did highlight some I find most important.

Some of the poems just flowed out of me, and some were much harder to write. I dove deep into the corners of my heart to connect back to some of those influential moments that shaped me. I never really miss being a kid, but while writing these poems it reminded me how sweet and tender those times really were.

A reflection on the places that brought me peace in times of chaos, and a feeling of closing chapters on the chaotic places I don't wish to ever return to.

This is A Poetic Plunge into the THEN that has gracefully (and at times not so gracefully) ushered me into the NOW.

Soledad

A solitary place.
A state of social isolation.
Both, a center piece on the day of my creation.
My mom was away from her home,
not familiar with places to roam.
My dad was working on a ship,
and the day of my birth he had to skip.
Thankful my dad's mom was there to hold her hand.
For her newest daughter she took a grandstand.
Even though it was tough,
my mom made it through.
A new chapter had begun,
this she knew.
Naming me after an actress she was so fond of.
Natalie Soledad, she dubbed me with love.
The older I get the more and more
I connect with this name.
Often finding solace in solitudes flame.
Allowing time and space with myself to fill me.
Floating in my heart's waters,
then from the outside noise I am free.

P.S. - Soledad

When my mom moved to the states, she went without any family. She was just 24 years old. My Dad was in the Navy and spent a lot of his time on the ship. The day that I was on my way to this Earth he was also on the ship. My Mom was without any of her immediate family and was accompanied to the hospital by my Grandma Gilmore as we called her. My dad's mom.

As an adult now, I can't even imagine how scary that must have been. First time birthing a child and doing so in a place you barely knew with new family. My Mom has always told me how supportive my Grandma Gilmore was, and that she was so grateful for all the help they offered in those first months when my mom was still adjusting.

Soledad is Spanish for loneliness, solitude or isolation. Now as an adult that just makes a lot of sense. The older I get, the more I realize that solitude is a core value of mine. I need alone time. I find my greatest ideas and feel most myself when I am alone or with nature. The name represents a part of me that I strive to honor in my life. The name is part of who I am, and what my heart longs for. Names don't have to mean a lot but mine means a lot to me now.

Recently my fiancé and I were talking about what my name would legally be after we married. I have heard that a lot of people drop their middle name to keep their maiden name in the mix. I just can't. I will legally have 4 names. I love it because they each mean something to me.

They each have a big part in my story.

Momma

She went through a lot,
but her heart never stopped.
She followed it to a faraway land,
soon holding her baby girl in two hands.
She's always been hard working.
Pushing through tough times that left her hurting.
Often wearing a thick suit of armor.
The inside of her heart is much warmer.
She's seen and learned so many things,
sharing them with me always gave me new wings.
From day one she encouraged my wildest dreams.
Helping me swim through life's crazy streams.
She's always been my biggest fan,
even while working with an adjusted plan.
Now I'm all grown up.
Sometimes we see life differently.
Approaching it all with patience and love gently.
We say love you lots always and forever.
And that will stand for whatever,
whenever,
wherever.

P.S. - Momma

Mother/Daughter relationships can be tough. Ours has been no different. We see the world very differently and have had our fair share of arguments. However, the older I get the more I recognize where her world view comes from, and why sometimes it's been so different than mine. Our life experiences were very different. Yet at the root of it all, we are both extremely passionate and emotional beings. When we believe in something, we really believe in it no matter what anyone else may think. The more I come into myself as an adult and reflect on the experiences that she had as a young adult, the more I am able to feel compassion for how she was able to deal with them. The coping tools that are so readily available to me now were not when she was young. Therapy was considered something for crazy people, and showing emotions was often viewed as a weakness. The values that were instilled in her were hard work and commitment to what was best for the family. She did and continues to do that relentlessly in her life.

She's dedicated her whole life to being a good mother regardless of the obstacles that came into her path. She persevered greatly and I will always admire that fully.

She's an animal, music and dance lover, all of which I know I got from her. The older I get and the more I learn about myself, the more I can relate to her and extend the compassion that I maybe lacked when I was younger.

Being a bonus mom now has opened my eyes wide to the great feat that is motherhood. I am forever grateful for her support of my wild dreams of becoming a dancer, and her now support as I tackle motherhood and new chapters in life. LYLAF Momma <3

LaLa

From the stories she tells,
to the way that she smells.
She's authentically she.
Little bits influenced me.
She loves a good piece of bread.
Her lips often painted red.
She's always wanted a yellow car,
even when she won't go far.
She feeds the crows as her own.
Many outfits she's hand sewn.
Years ago, she'd jump at the chance,
to enjoy a country line dance.
She's obsessed with keeping things clean.
I don't think I've ever seen her wear jeans.
She's an animal lover to the core.
Always worked hard to give her family more.
She loves her mom
and was the second youngest of eleven.
Most of them now rest peacefully in heaven.
She'll eagerly try to feed you all the time.
An act of love she doesn't view as a crime.
If she had it her way, we'd all live under the same roof.
Her joy the night before Christmas is proof.
Her heart is big even if she can't always show it.
The intentions are there with no adjustments or edits.
She taught me to feel pretty for myself and no one else,
what mattered the most is how we felt.
She often did my hair for school,
had me feeling so fresh and pretty darn cool.

P.S. - LaLa

A small glimpse into my grandmother.
She grew up in Corrientes, Argentina. Due to her large family and growing up in a small town with not much, my LaLa started working at a very young age. When my mother moved to the states and had me, my grandmother decided to leave Argentina to help her daughter. She helped my mom raise me. I remember her being strict and a neat freak, but I also remember playing checkers and cards with her. I am so grateful that I was able to have that time with her.

My LaLa was always doing something. Cleaning or moving furniture around. She never learned to speak much English at all. With very little schooling as a young girl, I'm amazed at how she was able to still make a life for herself in another country. She was a hard worker, (retired now) and almost nothing could stand in her way when she set her mind to something.

My LaLa is now battling dementia. It's such a weird disease. Things are different. Every day is new. For the most part she still remembers me and is only a bit confused when I FaceTime and remind her that I live on the other side of the world. Some days she's sad, but other days she's childlike and cracking jokes. I'll forever hang on to the memories of our time together when I was a kid, and equally to the times we get to laugh together now.

Big Bird

I remember watching them paint his feathers blue.
How my heart dropped, and perspective was new.
How could they do a terrible thing like that?
They locked him in a cage like an innocent lab rat.
My heart swollen with sadness,
the emotions overcame me.
It was the first time I felt pain
for someone other than me.
I wanted him to be free.
At the TV I pleaded.
My mom came in wondering what was wrong.
Tears poured out as I tried to be strong.
They rolled down my cheeks slowly as I cried.
I just wanted to help find him a place to hide.
Before actually knowing,
I already knew what empathy meant.
Compassion and tears were and still are my way to vent.

P.S. - Big Bird

I clearly remember the apartment that we lived in. I remember sitting on the carpet of the living room floor, and the tube-type of TV we had was on a short stand at just my height. "Follow That Bird" was the name of the movie. The story was about Big Bird being kidnapped and forced to perform for a circus to make them money. They painted him blue and made him sing a sad song in a cage.

I remember listening to that sad song and my eyes filled with tears. I can't remember crying for someone other than myself before that. I would only cry if I was tired or sometimes if I didn't get what I wanted. But this time I cried for the bird. I cried because he didn't have anyone to help him. I cried because they used his sadness to make money. Feeling true overwhelming compassion. Feeling deeply as a five-year-old for this bird that I loved so much. I mean, I was a fan of Sesame Street and so it felt like I knew him.

I am a highly sensitive person, and remembering this moment always confirms it for me. Feeling deeply for those that we care about, which at the time I cared about that big bird a lot. Showing signs at age five that I was emotionally built just a little different. Through my adult years, my sensitivity has sometimes felt like a hinderance. Yet, the more I dive into it and experience it fully, I realize how much of a superpower it is to feel so deeply, both for myself and for others.

Dance All Night

The day was full of white ruffles,
and really big pink bows.
Ready with a sprinkle of nerves,
but excited from head to toes.
The stage was foreign,
but somehow also calming.
I remembered my smile,
and found the audience charming.
My true self was shining like my tiny tap shoes.
Hearing the crowd cheer was truly the best news.
With starry eyes I watched the older girls dance away.
Excited to work hard and join them up there someday.
Back at home my adrenaline was flowing.
The camera was on me with cheeks still glowing.
It was almost midnight,
I wished to keep the day going with all my might.
From deep inside,
there was no calm in sight.
I knew with my whole heart,
that I could dance all night.

P.S. - Dance All Night

I started dancing when I was 5 years old. I was the one who asked my mom if I could take some dance classes. At that age, the local studio offered ballet and tap as a combo class, and I was so ready. The cute pink outfits and the shiny tap shoes completed my excitement perfectly. I just loved it. I remember loving the teacher that I had at that time. She was young, kind and smiled a lot. She was a ballerina herself, and I looked at her with starry eyes. At the end of that first year there was an annual recital. It would be my first time on a stage. The very beginning to a life full of stage moments to come. From what I remember, an overwhelming excitement filled me most of the day.

The feeling I'll never forget was the adrenaline that coursed through my body after the performance. A feeling of accomplishment. A feeling of pure joy. A feeling of elation that lasted hours after we had left the theater that day. My mom had rented a camcorder (a real 90's looking thing she had to prop up on her shoulder) to capture the magic. She continued filming when we got back home. Still in my costume, I am wearing a permanent smile. It was almost midnight, and I couldn't stop giggling. At some point I start dancing again in the kitchen, trying to recreate some of the moves I had seen the older girls do in the show. I couldn't wait to improve. I couldn't wait to keep dancing. I simply could have danced all night.

Play Birthday

I loved the feeling of performing,
and wanted to make it something reoccurring.
My birthday was on its way,
and I knew my friends would all be in the same place.
So, I organized some rehearsals at recess.
I took my favorite movie and added finesse.
It was the audience I wanted to impress.
Which was mostly made up of family I confess.
We played it out in my living room.
Remembered our lines as best we could.
We laughed, sang, and ended with a bang.
Needless to say, the crowd loved us.
Using my young leadership skills,
and willing friends was a plus.

P.S. - Play Birthday

My mom told me years later that my kindergarten teacher had told her that she felt I was a natural leader. She told my mom that I would often rally kids together to work on something extracurricular. I remember loving the feeling of having other kids my age to interact with. I remember feeling there were so many fun things that we could do together.

For my birthday that year I knew that I was inviting a handful of school friends to come celebrate with me at my house. I thought it would be so cool to put on a show for the parents. (My performance bug was raging.) And so, I gathered my friends during recess and mapped out a reenactment of my favorite Disney movie, Aladdin. The idea was also inspired by our kindergarten rendition of The Wizard of Oz. I don't remember much about how the actual performance went, but I remember us having a fun time preparing for it. I just wanted to keep performing in any way that I could.

Gymnastics

The sweat.
The conditioning workouts.
The soreness.
The pushing past "not wanting to."
The pain.
The tough love.
The persistence.
The chalky skin.
The bloody hand rips.
The tea bags to heal them.
The progress.
The tears.
The improvements.
The achievements.
The matching team leotards, and warm up suits.
The meets.
The team aspect.
The pushing through together.
This sport taught me a lot about life,
and helped mold me into
a stronger person than I ever thought I could be.

P.S. - Gymnastics

I was around 7 years old when I started doing gymnastics. I wanted to flip and fly the way I had seen the pros do on television. I thought to myself... "I can do that."

Dance was something that required hard work. Nonetheless, I was still young and so the work was not yet too strenuous. When I landed at the local gym for my first few practices, I was in shock. I was blown away by all the conditioning drills that we needed to get done before we could play on the bars or walk on the beam. Looking back, I know that my coaches pushed me because they saw potential in me.

I had already acquired some flexibility through dance and the grace in my dancing helped when I needed to stand tall and present softness in my hands and arms. I worked hard both in gymnastics and dance for a few years, but at some point, the schedules began to conflict with one another. My mom asked which one I wanted to continue with... I chose dance. I didn't know it at the time, but they really go together. One helps the other, and vice versa. In gymnastics I gained a lot of strength both physically and mentally. Years later, I would return to gymnastics in high school with one of the best coaches/mentors I ever had.

Gymnastics shifted my perspective on what hard work was at a very young age. Don't get me wrong, conditioning sessions at dance got much harder as the years went on, but I was more mentally equipped because of my experience with gymnastics. I'm so grateful that I had the opportunity to try it and enjoy it the way that I did.

Clara

I remember the sheets of lined paper
held up by tiny push pins.
A board made of cork
displaying all the wins.
Every year this is how we found out
who would play what parts.
Sometimes what you wanted
otherwise, a dart to the heart.
Seeing peers I admired play certain roles before,
made me want to play the same ones just a little more.
One big year this dream came true indeed,
seeing my name in lines, I was to play one of the leads.
Excited for the costumes, and to learn my staging cues.
It would be the very first time
I'd perform in my point shoes.
Big shoes to fill indeed.
All eyes would be on me.
Some eyes were intertwined with gentle jealousy.
Some interactions not so friendly,
almost made me not want to do it at all.
Wanting to please your friends,
can be a downfall.
But they got over it,
and I got really excited.
A dream come true.
I couldn't fight it.

P.S. - Clara

The yearly tradition at my dance studio was to perform The Nutcracker. A winter project where most of the studio was involved including the teachers, and often parents too. It was an exciting time each year to find out what parts we would play.

I remember playing a small mouse, a toy soldier, a snow-flake, and then one year I got to play the lead girl Clara. I was nervous and felt a lot of pressure, but I was ready. I would get to dance in my point shoes which were newer to me, but I was ready. I was ready to take center stage. I floated through rehearsals on a happy cloud. No one could bring me down.

I remember I had to sleep in hair rollers the night before our first dress rehearsal. My stick straight hair just didn't want to stay curled. A sacrifice I was willing to make to ensure that those long ringlets would stay in place. I remember my whole family came to watch. I remember being gifted a bouquet of flowers afterwards. I remember we would get a crew neck sweatshirt every year and have the other cast members sign it with a Sharpie like a yearbook. I remember the Christmas spirit floating around the studio.

Last year, I took myself to see The Nutcracker live for the first time in many years, and I cried nostalgic tears just re-membering all the hard work and fun we had doing so all those years.

Emily

She loved dance just as much as we did.
Tony Bennet would have been her dream gig.
She led us with her heart, rhythm and soul.
Her kindness ended up taking a toll.
After many years,
the business was no longer thriving.
She was getting too old to keep on diving.
She couldn't get the support she needed.
To her doors closing, she reluctantly conceded.
Which left us dancing kids without a place to call home.
But the memory of that space
Will in my heart forever roam.

P.S. - Emily

Emily was the owner of the dance studio I danced at from age seven to fifteen. It was dance home for me, and the place where I met many of my friends during these influential years of my childhood. It was the studio that had the yearly Nutcracker tradition, and it's where I learned so much of what would later lead me into my professional dance career.

It was a safe space for me. Formative years for me both as a dancer, and a human. My base training was in Ballet, Tap and Jazz but they exposed us to other things like Hip Hop, Flamenco and Tumbling. My short gymnastics background came in handy here.

We were a little family, and when her doors were finally set to close, I felt lost. Where would I dance now? What would happen to all the friends that I made? There were other studios, but it would never be the same. I was just about to start High School. How would I navigate all the new without my comfy home base? I would figure it out I was sure... but I was so sad.

That next summer, I auditioned for the High School Cheer Squad. I figured for now, that was the closest I could get to dancing.

Baby on Board

I was just barely a teen,
trying to find my way around how life seemed.
Hormones a blaze,
I'd listen to them argue from afar.
The energy so dense,
even when they were apart.
I knew things weren't right.
Lots of floating bitterness and spite.
Then one day, she sat me down
and told me of her baby on board.
Flooded with fear and confusion,
I roared.
How could she possibly want to stay tethered
to this man?
One who continued to hurt her for such a long span.
She was a bit surprised by my reaction.
I didn't mean to hurt her,
but the idea of raising a kid in those conditions
felt like torture.
I didn't know how I would deal,
also scared of how I might feel.
So much time and room to worry.
In my mind I was already in a hurry.

P.S. - Baby on Board

I had just started the 8th grade when my mom delivered the news to me. There had already been a lot of conflict between her and her partner at the time. I was confused, I thought babies came when couples were extra happy. Or at least that's what I had seen in the movies. I had been an only child up until this point. I knew this baby would soon require a lot of attention. I could feel that my mom wasn't happy, but she told me this was what she wanted. I know now that my confusion came out as anger. She later shared that she wasn't expecting me to be so upset. I just didn't know what was to come.

My world would soon flip upside down, and I wasn't so great with big change. Truthfully, I was scared. I didn't know how to be a sister. I wasn't sure if I would be a good one. I had my "own things" to worry about. I was about to go into High School. New school, teachers and friends were ahead of me. My best friend from middle school was going to a different high school too. My dance studio had just closed for good. I was losing a lot of my comfort zones. But I put my big girl pants on and got a job at the neighborhood ice cream shop that next summer.

I helped my mom tie his shoes in the early mornings before they drove me to school. My motherly nature turned on extra high at a young age. My Mom had bigger things to worry about. Short maternity leave would land her back at work soon, and I tried my best to help. This was one of those times when life kind of did a fast forward on me, and I was pushed into a big new era before I felt ready. Now looking back, I'm so proud of us and how we all got through it together.

Little Light

I didn't know they would shine a light so bright.
A genuine love I couldn't fight.
Such sweet little hands,
sharper than I could have ever planned.
Started using the computer at just age two.
Somehow knowing exactly what to do.
The glue our family needed.
Brought us closer, completed.
Our focus shifted.
In many ways lifted.
Truly one of a kind.
I love hearing about how they work their mind.

P.S. - Little Light

Looking back to the day my mom told me I had a sibling on the way: I could have never imagined the love that would grow between us. When we taught them how to say sister (Hermana) they quickly started to spit out Mana.

Mana became one of my greatest titles.

Watching the growth in those first few years was fascinating. A being so smart, bright and full of light. The missing piece that brought our whole family together. My Mom, Grandma, Aunt and cousins united to care for this tiny being, and for the first time in a long while I felt the family feeling again.

The star that lit up my mom's dark period, and I could see that. We all needed each other. Even though I didn't know it at the time, that star would grow up to be a smart, loving, respectful human who would teach me a lot about this life. As well as becoming an integral part of my growth as a young adult.

I love you so much Adrián.

He Just Left

He.
Just.
Left.
It was like, from one day to the next.
I remember them having a fight,
it was sometime late at night.
I could hear it from my room,
it felt like just another day of doom.
In the morning,
the apartment looked different.
Things had shifted.
It was the straw that broke the camel's back,
neither one cutting anymore slack.
Two souls drifted far enough away,
one of them no longer wanted to stay.
And without a moment's notice,
He.
Just.
Left.
Leaving us no chance to protest.

P.S. - He Just Left

Yep.

From one day to the next, he was gone. The man that had been my "stepdad" (even though they were never married) left us in a very vulnerable time. A time with a whole new person in play. A time where I was becoming a young adult. A time when my mom really needed his help, but he just left.

I'm sure there were multiple reasons for his departure, but I just didn't have time to think about them or him for that matter. I blocked him out of my mind completely, and focused on helping at home as much as I could. I also decided to get busy with my own life. I filled up my days with things to do so as not to think about the mess and great depression that my mother was left with.

We pushed through. I kept my grades up and did my best in my extracurricular activities. It wasn't always easy, but we found our flow.

I knew my mom was hurting. So instead of contributing to the sadness, I got busy and starting teaching kids at a local dance studio as well. I wanted to find that thing I was good at since school wasn't really that. The teenage pieces were slowly starting to weave together.

Mana

I didn't know what I was gunna do.
I didn't know how to be a sister.
A big sister at that.
That comes with a lot of responsibility,
especially at fifteen.
I was old enough to help,
but I felt my biggest help
came from taking care of myself.
Making sure that I was straight,
so that my mom could manage the sadness
from the fact that stepdad went packing.
Wanting to protect them now.
That, my mother taught me how.
She showed me love and care,
now her heart shattered and bare.
I did my best to find all the little pieces,
and pour them back tenfold
into that little human's creases.
It made me grow up fast.
Between two jobs and the baby, sometimes I was last.
I think she saw me more grown up than I felt.
Playing tough, still at times my insides would melt.
I didn't know how to be a sister yet,
but as the years went on,
a little light in my heart grew.
Sometimes that little light
was the only thing that got me through.
I started new traditions,
and found ways to get into their heart.
Learning to be a big sister
has been one of my greatest arts.

P.S. - Mana

I had no idea how it would all unfold. I didn't know how to be a good sister. But I learned and am still learning. We have a big age gap which I feared would interfere with our bond. But as life develops for both of us, I see how being a sister has incredible perks. We can talk about things a bit differently. We can relate to both being children from the same Mom. We are both pursuing freelance type of work and have no desire to conform to conventional means of work. We have a lot more in common than I ever thought we would. They bring me calm when I am not and remind me that life is not as serious as I often take it.

Being a sister is like being part of a really cool club that only a select few know what it feels like. It feels important and exciting. It feels great to be able to share life lessons I've learned along the way. It feels rewarding when they overcome something or achieve something they are proud of. It feels amazing to know that they will always be my sibling no matter what. That there is this thread that connects us no matter where in the world we may be.

Contrary to my first beliefs, being a big sister has been one of life's greatest gifts, and I wouldn't trade it for the world.

High School

I spent a lot of time at the school.
Lots of activities and friends, I felt cool.
I cheered on my friends,
and flipped on the balance beam.
The yearly talent show was a highlighted dream.
I was part of a group that made the freshmen
feel supported.
Our teachers cared about students assorted.
There was even a group dedicated to sexual safety.
We taught the underclassmen how to engage safely.
There were friends that supported,
and ones that hurt me.
Teachers that really believed in all that I could be.
The greatest lessons were through my interactions
with other people.
I enjoyed it but wouldn't necessarily order a sequel.

P.S. - High School

I was a bit bullied in elementary school. I was a bit envied in middle school. But when I got to high school, I felt excited. I was ready to meet new people and have different types of classes to choose from. I wanted to absorb as much goodness as I could both academically and socially. Unlike many, my High School experience was a great one. I enjoyed engaging in groups and sports that kept me busy. I had a good group of friends. Some classmates I had known since kindergarten. I remember a lot of the teen feelings. Boys and boyfriends feeling really important, and even though I wasn't dancing much, I was able to make up for it when I made the cheer squad. I loved Friday night football games and the winter gymnastics season. Pep-rallies and school dances were so fun to me.

I was craving independence. I got my license just as soon as I could. I felt ready to take on life. Haha, I had no idea what was ahead. In the last two years of High School, I endured a lot of emotional blows. Betrayal from friends and boyfriends along with that feeling of "what happens next?" What happens when I'm done with school? What will I do? What do I want to do?

I was so ready to grow up. I realize now, I had so much time to do that. I am so glad I have some great memories of that time before all the adulting kicked in.

A Cold stone

I had a boss named Lou.
He showed me what I needed to do.
We made ice cream from scratch.
He let me sample a little from every batch.
We mixed a batter that would press into cones.
I remember how the sweet smell
would stick to my bones.
We would sing a little jingle when tips landed in the jar.
I was making my own money, something new by far.
I saved up enough money for my first prom dress.
It felt good to keep my mom from any added stress.
I worked three summers in a row,
and gained extra pounds to the core.
It taught me a lot about being on time
and staying consistent.
Things that later helped me stay focused and persistent.

P.S. - A Cold stone

My first job. The first paychecks that I could call my own. The first money that I would save up for something I really wanted. The first boss and group of co-workers that I would learn to collaborate with. The first big bags of trash that I would carry, and the first time I would genuinely feel tired from something that wasn't already a passion of mine.

Coldstone had this quirky gimmick that when a customer would tip us, we would sing a short jingle in return. I must say I think it really worked. Although I don't remember how many tips I made exactly, I remember the big smiles that would come during and after each jingle. After jingle 200 or so of course I was over it, but it was part of the job. I assumed the responsibility of keeping the tip joy alive.

My boss Lou was a jolly man that was passionate to keep the store thriving. He taught me how to make the ice cream, and waffle cones, and he did it all with a big smile. I don't think I could have asked for a better first job. It was walking distance from home, and ice cream ... yes ice cream just makes people happy.

First Love

It was the first time I felt love, and comfort
in the same person.
He came at a time when I expected things to worsen.
He was a smiling ray of sunshine that parted my clouds.
We ran in similar, yet different crowds.
He was smart, fun, and in it for the long haul.
He was also just the right amount of tall.
He had big plans for us.
I had other ones that we needed to discuss.
We all felt he was headed in the right direction.
My mom saw us together as perfection.
But I had dreams and goals
that weren't part of the docket.
I was eager to take off on my independent rocket.
We had a special time that I'll never forget.
He loved me deep and I'm so glad that we met.

P.S. - First Love

My first real feelings of love came in my second year of high school. I was still adjusting to the sister thing, and sometimes having a crying baby at home was not easy. My then boyfriend and his family welcomed me with open arms. They cared for me as one of their own, and I felt it. I felt included and loved. He was a very smart young man who had his goals set. He told me that he wanted to marry me when I was done with school.

This was so overwhelmingly beautiful yet terrifying at the same time. He knew what he wanted out of this life, and I didn't yet. I felt we were two birds flying in different directions. I had the feeling that if I passed up on this kind of love, it may never find me again. But something deep down told me that it would, and that when it did, it would feel just right.

I let him fly away with tears in my eyes, and fear in my heart. Unsure if that love would ever return, but sure there was more love to be found. So, I went in search of all the life that was yet to be found.

Summer Love

We fell for each other on a warm summer night.
Friends before that,
we fought the attraction with might.
It was comfortable, familiar,
but somehow also a thriller.
You were the jock that shared my love for athletics.
A major perk was witnessing your phonetics.
You were the guy that kept everyone laughing.
You were never too scared of dancing.
I was a fan of your summer playlist.
You made me a mixtape I couldn't resist.
Things ended up taking a really weird turn,
one that felt like a third-degree burn.
But I learned in that moment,
that you wanted something contrasting.
And from our friendship I started fasting.
It always stung a bit to see you with her.
Senior year was a quite a big blur.
Years later we managed to stay in touch,
mutual friends kept us as such.
Until one day you met your wife.
Over time you started a whole new life.
One I wasn't a part of anymore,
but I was truly happy for you at the core.
Now you're a dad, and we don't speak at all,
but I smile knowing that you're having a ball.

P.S. - Summer Love

He was a jock. Baseball. A lefty pitcher. He was the life of the party. He loved dancing and rapping out his favorite tunes at the time.

He was my friend for a while before that. The summer before junior year came, sparks flew. We felt things that had maybe been brewing up the years before that. We rolled with it and had a fun summer.

On the night of our first homecoming dance, I found him kissing one of my good friends.

OUCH! It was the first heart that broke mine, and I didn't like it. They went on to date for two more years after that, which pained me to see but I had to accept. I played it "cool," and told him we could still be friends. Those were some serious lies that I told myself at the time, but I learned from them. I learned that I wasn't cool, and that my friends would soon change.

Around the same time, I was dancing with a group outside of school, and I plunged into this group with brute force. I needed some new energies in my life, and this group of artists was just what I needed.

A New Breed

I was nervous, and out of my comfort zone.
I decided to take a chance on my own.
My hopes were not high, as I didn't know this tribe.
A very talented team with an infectious vibe.
I didn't know what to expect,
but the audition was pretty direct.
We learned some moves and performed them at our best.
The panel of judges would decide the rest.
I didn't quite know that kind of adrenaline rush,
but that was the first of many to come in flush.
I waited days that felt like months to hear a final answer,
wondering if it was possible to be that chosen dancer.
Seeing my name in the blue light of the screen,
was the first time in a while I really felt seen.
A group to belong to outside of school.
The addition to my schedule made me feel hella cool.
What I didn't know was that these people
would later become family.
Friends.
Supporters.
Motivators.
Northwest majesty.
Eternally grateful for the time that we shared.
Late nights.
Long chats.
People who really cared.

P.S. - A New Breed

I had heard about this audition from a fellow cheerleader at school. She was also teaching at the dance studio that I worked at, and she said, "You should just go with no expectation and see what happens." So, I went.

My first audition since the small in-studio ones for the annual Nutcracker. A room full of people I didn't know, which was scary but maybe made it easier to focus on myself. I danced my little heart out that day, and I remember how exhilarated I felt afterwards. A little bit of that "Dance All Night" feeling all over again. Now, I was invested and determined to dance with this incredible group. The level was high, but I was up for the challenge. The rehearsals would be in the evenings at a studio about 45 minutes from my home. But when they invited me in, I was determined to make it work. I needed a change of pace, and the fact that it was something outside of school, and away from some of those people that had hurt me sealed the deal.

This talented group of people quickly became my new dance family. We did a lot together and hung out both in and outside of the studio. Dancers at my level with a heart to match. Endless laughs and good times I'll never forget. Being a part of this group was also the first time I was exposed to other dancers that were moving to LA and making careers for themselves as performers. This was the spark I needed to send me into motion for what would be the beginning of my professional dance career. I am forever grateful to the organizers and dancers for believing in me. They supported me through those years and many more after that. I could have never known the greatness and blessings that were coming when I decided to audition that day.

Wisdom Teeth

I remember being awake the whole time.
Lots of crunching and cracking,
an in-my-mind grind.
I knew it had to be done.
I was ready for swollen fun.
When I got home, two letters awaited me.
Two rejection letters from schools not meant to be.
Ouch! to both my heart and my mouth.
I wasn't sure this day could go more south.
At first, my heart sunk thinking,
"You couldn't even do that."
I wanted to curl up and become a house cat.
But in a way, I was also a bit relieved.
Now no one else's dreams to be achieved.
Time to put mine at the forefront.
Time for a dream chasing treasure hunt.
Putting myself into gear,
trying to disintegrate the fear.
I'd set myself up for my greatest success.
Excited to see how it would all progress.

P.S. - Wisdom Teeth

I almost didn't write about this story because it seemed slightly insignificant, but the more I thought about it, the more I realized how pivotal of a moment this was for me. Not because of my swollen mouth, but because of the liberation that those rejection letters brought me on that day.

Part of me thought that getting into college would set me on the "normal" path that I was "supposed" to take. As soon as I read those words of redirection, I knew deep in my gut that I was supposed to do more. That it wouldn't be mapped out in a curriculum for me, but that I was supposed to grab the reigns myself, and make that shit happen on my own.

I was a bit confused (or maybe that was the pain meds,) but I almost pretended to be sadder than I was. I remember feeling a slight relief that I wouldn't have to do what all the other kids were doing. I remember thinking "this is my chance to run and grab all the crazy ideas that I have been seeing in my head lately."

I'm glad my mom and teachers pushed me to apply to college, because otherwise I may have wondered "what if?" But I was free of that feeling now, and more focused to find out how I would go about my next chapter without the curriculum of a university to get me through it. I didn't know how it would happen just yet, but I knew where I wanted to go.

I now realize how much wisdom that day brought me for my future.

California Dreamin'

I was dreaming of the sun.
I was dreaming of the beach.
I was dreaming of a stage.
A dream I could only dream to reach.
Under the bright lights I dreamt
of dancing the night away.
Looking out into a sea of people
swimming through an emotional array.
So many places I dreamt to see,
really quite unsure of how it all could be.
All I knew, was the love that flowed from my heart.
One that always allowed me to keep going for my art.
The path was narrow, and I knew what I had to do.
Keep hustling hard while keeping my eyes
on the new view.
Open up my mind to the possibility of it all.
Keep pushing my limits, while standing tall.
I had to trust myself, and the dreams I had dreamt.
Stay focused on what I knew as the present.

P.S. - California Dreamin'

Now my eyes were set on the prize. I knew where I wanted to go, but I was young and broke and unsure how to make it all happen. My mom was working hard to keep the boat afloat, and so I knew that if I wanted to do it then I would have to figure out how to do it myself.

I worked hard for the next year and saved up what I thought was a lot of money. (Haha, it wasn't so much money.) I paired up with another girl from my dance group that was also intending to move to LA. We agreed to be room-mates and begun the hunt for apartments.

Now looking back, the fact that I mobilized this grand move mostly on my own, at age 19, is wild to me. I was de-termined, and nothing could get in my way. With stars in my eyes, and dance in my heart, I was ready to take the leap.

A moment of gratitude here for my mom who really sup-ported me and told me to go do it. She said she had always wanted to be an actress, but the cards hadn't played out for her. She said she didn't want me to look back and have the regret of not trying. So, I told her to give me two years to see what would happen. If after two years I was unsatisfied, I would come back home to go back to school and follow "the plan" that so many had.

Coffee Bucks

I didn't even like coffee.
It was a whole new world for me.
I learned about the plant into beans, into coffee process.
It helped me appreciate every cup a bit more, I confess.
It would be my ticket to the sunny state.
Whatever needed to be done, there was no debate.
Clocking in before the sun,
espresso shots had me spun.
Learning all the different drink combinations,
understanding the details of the different stations.
Sometimes long lines, and grumpy caffeine feigns.
Giving them what they needed by any and all means.
And often a customer who needed an ear to listen.
In between orders, I'd pause for a quick intermission.
I scrubbed floors, and cleaned bathrooms not my own,
but it all quickly became just like a second home.
It was a place where everybody knew my name.
A place where for just a few moments
we were all the same.

P.S. - Coffee Bucks

Well, you can imagine by the title where I decided to work my first year after high school. That famous Seattle founded space. A place that I didn't really know much about before I started working there. I didn't even drink coffee. I thought it tasted so bitter and gross. Of course, after some time, and many white chocolate mochas later that slowly changed.

The job was a suggestion from a fellow dancer who had also made the move to LA. She told me that once I had worked there for a bit, and was well trained, that the company would be able to transfer me directly to a store in LA. THAT was my golden ticket. To make the money now, but keep making the money when I got there, with little to no gap in the bank account. I officially had a plan!

Waking up super early was a new thing for me. It was already so hard for me to get up in the mornings for school. But this time there was a big reason to do so, and that overshadowed the swollen eyes that didn't want to open. I quickly befriended a triple (sometimes quad) shot of espresso over ice and got to work.

Despite the early mornings and grumpy caffeine feigns, the thing I remember most were the relationships that were built in that space. The regular customers that would chat with me while I made their coffee, or the co-workers with big dreams of their own who were following a similar path. We were a cute group of passionate caffeine distributors, and some of them I still keep up with. I am forever grateful for the friend who suggested it, and that company for allowing me the space to have something steady and still flexible while I pursued some of my biggest dreams.

Leaving the nest

It never quite felt like leaving,
a little more like proceeding.
To explore a dream that I wanted.
Exciting things all sugar frosted.
Many reminded me how hard it would be,
but I was ready to take it in with glee.
I sought out to make plans with a couple friends.
Inspired by our craft, we were sure we'd have a blast.
Ready to see what a new place would bring,
we locked in our first apartment and got into the swing.
Saying bye to family was not as hard as I thought,
but in the coming months I thought of them a lot.
I didn't know much besides that I wanted to dance,
everything else I would take by chance.

P.S. - Leaving the nest

And off I went! Exactly a year after graduation, it was time to pack up and go. The apartment in LA was set and had been advanced by my roommate and her mom. I trusted them and didn't really care where I lived as long as there was warm water and a roof. Crazy that I never saw my first apartment in person until the day that I moved in.

The studio I had been working at part-time threw me a small going away party. Many parents reminded my mom of how hard this journey could really be, but none of that mattered. I couldn't hear the words they were saying. I was ready and laser focused. At the time, I drove a small Dodge Neon that used to be my aunts. I packed that baby to the brim (which wasn't much,) and with my at-the-time boyfriend drove down the west coast of the United States.

We drove for two days all the way down to Los Angeles, California. I remember we stopped somewhere about halfway to sleep in a small motel, but I couldn't tell you where or what the name of it was. My thoughts were only on getting there. Driving through the south of Oregon, and the north of California was so scenic. It was a long ass drive that I never made again after that day. It was time to start new, and with only my small car full of belongings I did just that.

No time to sleep

There were times where there was no time to sleep.
The day would move so quick,
and in the sun would creep.
Making coffee through the early mornings,
rehearsing into the late evenings.
Sometimes performing at night.
Those were the nights my sleep and I would fight.
It was a time of constant push.
At times my body was mush.
I didn't know quite where I would land,
but just woke up every day
to take a grandstand.
To live another day,
full of all the things I wanted to stay.
To keep going down the road I chose.
At each checkpoint, I'd just strike a pose.
Making the best of each obstacle and turn,
lighting my own fire, and watching it burn.

P.S. - No time to sleep

One of the things I remember the most about my first years in LA, was the struggle that was trying to find the dance/life balance. I needed the schedule flexibility to be available for opportunities as they came. (which was often random and last minute) But I also needed the financial stability to pay my bills. I wanted to say yes to all the dance opportunities that came, and at the time most of them were unpaid. It was like doing an internship. Learning the lay of the land. Creating relationships with teachers and choreographers that I wanted to work with. It felt a bit chaotic. Every day was new with fresh possibilities. I had to keep the job to keep the apartment, to stay dancing my heart out in LA.

However, there were nights when I was asked to perform in a show, (usually at a nightclub somewhere in Hollywood) and the show wouldn't start until 11:00 pm. I would be out of there by 1:30/2:00 am and then head home to shower and freshen up before leaving the house at 4:00 to be at work by 4:30.

Yeah. I'm still not quite sure how I made it through some of those nights into mornings, but I knew that my quad espresso over ice awaited me, and I was up for the task. I remember taking naps at the desk in the backroom instead of eating on my thirty-minute break. I remember getting off work around 12:30pm the next day and crash landing in my bed around 1:00. Then, I would take a nap just before my alarm went off to get ready for dance class or my shift at the dance studio in the evening.

I'm proud to say I lived to tell the story. I would sometimes stand behind the coffee counter, half asleep, dreaming of what it would look and feel like to dance on those huge stages someday.

First Attempt

A friend of mine who was oh-so kind,
one who had learned the ropes,
also full of hopes.
She pointed me in the direction of my dreams,
saw and nurtured my hungry light beams.
At the time I didn't know it,
but these small steps sent me into orbit.
She was consistent even when farther away,
and always helped me find my way.
On this particular day, she sent me to an audition.
One that would help bring my dreams to fruition.
A company that would represent me,
and take me to places only my heart could see.
I got what I came for.
I wanted it with every pore.
I couldn't have done it without that first attempt.
From there I could flow with fear exempt.

P.S. - First Attempt

I really had no idea what I was doing when I moved to LA. I wish there would have been a crash course on how to start when you get there with a heart full of passion, but no real knowledge on how to become a freelance professional dancer.

Luckily, I had friends. Friends that were doing similar things a few years ahead of me. One of those friends told me I needed an agent that would work for me. They would be the company that would represent me. They would help me not only get information about auditions but would handle the legal and financial details of the jobs that would hopefully come soon.

It made sense, and I was just eager to have someone help me. That same friend also told me about an audition that was happening soon. The agents would hold auditions every so often to cast new dancers to represent. I jumped at the chance, and to my surprise, I was signed by my first agency just six months after making the big move. I want to say I got lucky, not because I wasn't talented, but because the agents didn't hold very many of those castings. I just happened to have a friend that led me right to one.

Those types of synchronicities felt like they came from the dance angels that were watching over me to help make my ride just a little smoother.

Work Study

You could always feel the energy,
as soon as you walked through the doors.
A vibrant space filled with sweaty hearts,
and creative outpours.
I worked behind the tiny desk
signing students in with pen and paper.
Creatives with endless style and flavor.
Some of them became mentors of mine,
others incredible friends I wasn't sure I would find.
It was a place where I learned
so much more than just dance.
Into the industry I had a broader glance.
It was a place to call home.
Behind those walls my creativity could roam.
Forever grateful for that space,
for jumpstarting my career with grace.

P.S. - Work Study

I found out through the grapevine that the world-re-nowned Millennium Dance Complex offered a work-study program. At that time, you could work hours at the front desk in exchange for a certain number of classes per week. I would have one short shift per week, but that helped me get more training in without having to break the bank. Compared to now, everything was much cheaper, but those were times when my barista budget was tight. Every little bit helped.

The extra time I spent at the studio made it feel like home. I slowly got to know more teachers and choreographers and made some friends behind the desk too. It was a way of connecting with the community outside of the actual dancing part.

I really enjoyed my time there. I also built relationships that are still present in my life decades later. After a few years behind the desk, I went on to working there as a teacher. I worked there in one capacity or another for all 16 years that I lived in LA.

I am forever grateful for all the opportunities that Millennium Dance Complex gave me.

Car Trouble

My luck with cars was not the best.
It truly became one of life's biggest tests.
Every time I felt a glow up,
I quickly got knocked down.
In a big city like LA,
it was tough to get around.
From hand-me-downs to beaters,
I couldn't seem to find any keepers.
I've been in accidents both small and large,
and paid one too many a service charge.
I rode a two-wheel express for almost three years.
Eternally grateful to my peers,
who helped push me through the tears,
and eventually switch gears.
Although I was in the best shape I've ever been,
being thankful for my working legs was really the win.
I gave my best mentally and physically,
trying to be the best that I possibly could be.

P.S. - Car Trouble

As this poem starts off, my luck with cars was not the best. Time after time, I was met with obstacles concerning my car(s). At some point one of my cars had been totaled, and I didn't have the insurance coverage or funds to repair it. So, I bought myself a bicycle. I rode that thing all over LA for three years, and man was that a tough time in my life.

Not only was I physically exhausted from biking to and from dance classes or events, but I was mentally drained with what seemed like no end to a bad patch of luck. I had one transmission go out on me. I was in one smaller accident that left my car unrepairable. Then I was involved in one bigger accident, which thankfully no one was hurt in. Lastly, one of my cars was stolen right from the street that I lived on!!! Can you believe that? It was found days later completely stripped of all its parts.

The perseverance was real, and eventually I bought my first car which was with me for over 5 years. I feel I finally broke the streak of bad luck, but I learned so much along the way. I drive so differently now. I guess in a way I'm grateful for the journey. But I know that I don't ever want to learn those lessons that way again. Drive safe out there y'all.

Welcome to the Jungle

It truly felt like one.
Animals of every kind.
Most hunting the same prey.
A magic job they hoped to find.
Looking to each other with smiles before and after,
but during the hunt, compete they'd rather.
The rooms filled with tension even without mention.
The judges judged with business-driven intention.
Now the animals came for their prey,
fighting through a regular workday.
The effects are vast from staying in fight or flight,
living there too long, simply dims your light.
But sometimes you wanna fight,
and sacrifice a lot for the chance to fly.
The chance to make your dreams come true.
That's when we'll journey the jungle
through and through.

P.S. - Welcome to the Jungle

LA truly felt like a jungle at times. It took me a long while to adjust. I'm not sure if I ever fully adjusted to the lifestyle, but I found what worked for me and followed my instincts along the way. Every artist was hunting their next prey (job.) Auditions often felt primal and intense. The smiles were sometimes fake and loaded with tension. Those conducting the auditions were often stone faced and needed to be particular about who they chose.

You usually left an audition not knowing why they cut you or what you could do better next time. Most auditions were like walking through a maze. You might observe who they are keeping, but you aren't sure why, and you aren't sure if you may also be a good fit. This leaves you doubting yourself and your craft. Sometimes you have to put your feelings aside, and fight for what you believe can be yours. You don't have time to overthink yourself or your art when you're in the moment.

Hunt for what you need. If you get it, enjoy it. And then start the process all over again. Exhausting but exhilarating. This part keeps people wanting more. Wanting to decode the formula and conquer the jungle somehow. Some are successful often and some only eat occasionally. It all comes in waves, and seasons of sorts.

You've got to have tough skin and keep pushing through. Your tribe (support system) is the biggest key. Surround yourself with those that lift you up and make you feel safe in the jungle.

Comparing

There were so many people,
with so much talent.
We all wanted the same thing.
Toward our big dreams we hoped to swing.
There was intimidation,
that I now know stemmed from inspiration.
We each had something unique,
even in the weeks that we may have felt weak.
I realize now,
comparing was a waste of time.
We would all get our chance
when it was our time.

P.S. - Comparing

This is something I know so many people, but especially artists go through. We often compare ourselves to other artists, and usually that stems from us being inspired by their work. They have something that we find awesome or beautiful, and that turns us to wonder if we ourselves have some of those same qualities in our art. If we are also in fact good enough or worthy enough of accomplishing our goals and dreams.

When I was younger these feelings would overwhelm me. I didn't know how to process them. There were times when comparison and jealousy got the best of me. I was only hurting myself. I was only bringing myself further down by trying to find similarities between me and someone who was not me. I later learned a phrase that has stayed with me since.

"I am the only me, and that is my superpower."

The crazy thing is there really is only one me and there will never be another.

Nowadays, when I start to hear the comparison loop from that little voice, (because it still creeps in from time to time) I try to redirect it towards "What qualities does that person have that I would like to learn from or in some way be inspired by?"

Rejection

They would never say "No, you're not it."
Hours of preparation,
leading to maximum exertion.
It would take just one quick second
to utter those two words kindly.
"Thank You" they'd say.
All I could hear was,
"You're not special enough."
"You don't have what we need."
Never knowing why not,
even when I felt I had succeeded.
Better luck next time, I guess.
For that day...
The End and on to the next.

P.S. - Rejection

In the beginning of my career this was something I had to get used to. There were so many times where I wasn't what they were looking for. I would get myself ready with hair and make-up, choose an outfit that I thought would catch the panels attention, and hopefully get some time to stretch and warm- up when I got there. Sometimes, all of this would take place before 10:30 in the morning. It was a bit of a different era for dance, and in-person auditions were a very regular thing. They wanted to see what you could do right in front of them. I felt it was also a test of pressure and perseverance if by chance you messed up a step or two.

But almost every audition had one thing in common. After you danced, they would have us stand in a straight line. After their immediate deliberation, the panel of judges would have an appointed person that would come to the line and whisper in each person's ear. You would either hear "Thank You" or "Please Stay." Please stay meant of course they wanted to see you dance again, and Thank You was so kind of them, but it stung. They were being grateful, and I had this ball in my stomach that I would hold onto until (depending on the week) I was able to break down and cry in my car, or hopefully make it all the way home before that happened.

I want to tell you that the Thank You's got easier, but honestly, they didn't. The more I worked and the more experience I had, the less I wanted to hear it. But what I can tell you is that I realized that often when a job wouldn't go the way I wanted, there was another one around the way not far that I wasn't expecting. And maybe, just maybe, that rejection was my redirection to the gigs that were truly meant for me.

Self-Doubt

It starts with us.
Maybe inspired by what we see, hear and feel.
But ultimately it starts with us.
It's something to discuss.
No one else to blame.
Sometimes just a dim inner flame.
Missing belief.
Truly a joy thief.
It deeply clouds the mind.
Inspiration harder to find.
Taking us in circles,
creating more hurdles.
We must let go of the doubt,
and dig deep into the trust.
Let our art not be rushed,
or our own self-belief crushed.

P.S. - Self-Doubt

I wonder how it is that we lose belief in ourselves in the first place. I know for me it often comes from outside influences. Seeing others doing things I also want to be doing or loving the way they do it, and somehow wishing for something similar for myself.

But the truth is, it's impossible to have something similar when two artists are so uniquely different. Even when they are making the same kind of art there is no way that both could ever be the same. Each person has a unique artistic fingerprint. The thing I try to always remember is that no one can ever take that away from me, and it is only my belief in that fingerprint that keeps it alive and thriving.

It is only with that belief that my confidence in my art can grow. No one outside of me can tell me what my art should or shouldn't be. We must be our biggest cheerleaders. We can't wait for anyone else to cheer us on. The belief we have in our art is what keeps the stream of creativity flowing.

Give me two years

I said, "Give me two years."
Let's see how it goes.
Maybe it doesn't work.
Maybe it flows.
I couldn't have predicted the hardships that awaited me,
there were so many things I wanted to see.
Through liars, and break ups,
early mornings, and car troubles.
My passions stayed consistent,
and then my drive doubled.
I was determined to meet the goals that I had set,
even when there was no light in the tunnel yet.
I fought harder than I even knew was possible.
Kept faith in myself and did what was honorable.
My world kept spinning, and I held on tight.
Not letting any goals out of my sight.
Two years flew by like smoke in the wind.
I was still certain that I had to win.

P.S. - Give me two years

I mentioned this before, but when I was leaving Seattle, I told my mom, "Just give me two years to see what might happen." When that two-year mark was creeping up, I had still not booked any big jobs. I was still working at the bucks. I couldn't quite see the light at the end of the tunnel. I wasn't sure if I could really do it. But like straight out of a movie, at right about that two-year mark I was asked to audition for a well-known artist. All of this on the same day that I had a court appointment for a traffic ticket that I got for not stopping at a stop sign completely. (Insert eye roll emoji) I thought "Once again, just my luck."

How would I ever book a job if life kept life-ing? Then on my way home I got a call from the choreographer. She said they hadn't found what they were looking for at the audition. She asked me to come to her house and learn the choreography in her living room. She said she would film it and send it to the artist for review.

Guess what?!
I got my first big job just shortly after my two-year mark of living in LA. More on that soon...

The Light in the Tunnel

And finally,
a light appeared.
Just after two years.
It's disappearance I feared.
I was afraid I couldn't do it.
Anticipating with my dreams a split,
but a new flame was lit.
Butterflies emerged in my stomachs pit
one afternoon when I received the call
that would change it all.
Familiar voices asked me if I wanted to go on tour.
The joy was pure, of this, I was sure.
To travel the world and see new places.
Leaving behind little bits of my dream traces.
There would be stages to light up,
everything started to speed up.
As we prepared for a six-month promo run,
I was giddy for all the work, and mounds of fun.
I couldn't have imagined how magical it would really be,
but my heart was open, and full of glee.
It was time to tackle my first big job.
All my heart could do was throb.

P.S. - The Light in the Tunnel

Two long years... that kind of zoomed by. It felt like a long time, but also flashed by in the blink of an eye. I was just about to start getting impatient when I received this call from the choreographer. I wanted to work as a dancer so badly, but at this point I wasn't sure if that would ever happen.

This opportunity came at the "perfect" time. Relieving me of the doubt and reminding me that sometimes things come just as and when they are supposed to. I remember being in the car and seeing the call come in.

I pulled over.
Both choreographers were on the phone and asked me,
"Do you want to go on tour with us?"
Time slowed down, and a smile wiped over my face.
"Of course!" I remember blurting out.

Not only would it be the first time that I would work professionally as a dancer, but we would be traveling internationally to places like Mexico, Greece, China and Japan. Holy wow!!
With stars in my eyes, I was ready.

Tokyo Seaweed

As I gazed out into the open air,
all I saw was arms and heads floating
in what felt like a Tokyo Sea breeze.
Their bodies pressed close,
dancing together like seaweed on the ocean floor.
I starred hypnotically for a few more moments,
until I was given the five minutes to show warning.
My head spun,
as my insides turned.
I flipped my grip and took some deep breaths.
It was showtime in Tokyo.
Roughly eighty thousand sent my heart pounding.
But I smiled.
I had waited twenty-one years,
and two long ones leading up.
I was ready.
Or at least my heart was,
and hopefully my body would follow suit.
If not, hopefully the seaweed would catch me.

P.S. - Tokyo Seaweed

Summer Sonic was the name of the festival, and it was an outdoor show for close to 80,000 people. The biggest crowd I had ever seen let alone performed for. My nerves were on 100, but I was mostly excited. I felt that excitement rise as we walked toward the stage. When we were set in our places to start, I looked out at the crowd for the first time. It looked like seaweed swaying gracefully at the bottom of the ocean floor. I couldn't see faces, just feeling. A feeling of "Wow, this is insane!" and "I'm so ready to get out there."

Our show intro started with some big flags that were hard to maneuver, and I just remember going over the movements to make sure that I didn't mess up the first song. The music started and I looked out into the ocean of humans one last time while nervously smiling. It was time to start my career as a professional dancer.

And so, it all began...

The tour was the called "The Best Damn Thing," and it truly was the best damn thing to happen to me. I learned so much about how to be a working dancer, while tackling the traveling element at the same time. I saw and stayed on my first tour bus as well as appearing on television for the first time as a professional dancer. The choreographers/mentors became family, and they helped little 21-year-old me all the way through. I am eternally grateful to them for the chance and the guidance in that crazy year of 2007.

Back to the rind

The big dream come true ended quickly.
I could feel the bank account getting prickly.
It was time to go back to the grind.
This time less beans, and a little more rind.
Energizing juices to fill up the active souls.
Time to fill in the blanks and set some new goals.
Fallen fruit on the floor made it sticky like a fly trap,
and me the fly looking for a new map.
Trying to keep my hopes high,
sometimes forcing a look so spry.
I knew this wasn't my final place to be,
yearning to drift with more Tokyo seaweed.
I sanitized many blenders,
while on the dance floor meeting contenders.
It was just another phase in this chapter of my book.
Persistence and perseverance were the approaches
that I took.

P.S. - Back to the rind

After that first big job, I think I had the impression that magically more jobs would be soon to follow. I felt like I had opened the floodgates, and now I just needed to wait for the flood. But the flood didn't come. I had the most money in my bank account I had seen so far in life, and I celebrated by spending it. I gifted my friend's big birthday presents and took us on fun adventures. I felt they had supported me so greatly that I wanted to repay them in some way.

It was an amazing year or so, but quickly the funds started to run dry. I could see that number in my account dwindling, and I knew it was time to stop waiting for the flood. I had to get myself another job. Something that I thought somewhere in my young mind that I would never have to do again.

I didn't want to go back to the bucks. I was so drained from that place. I needed a new place with new energy. Instead of caffeinated beverages, I turned to smoothies, and juices of all kinds. After I got the job, I realized that the customers were so different. I normally encountered endorphin filled smiles after their workouts. Or a quick stop for an afternoon boost during their busy errands. I learned about wheatgrass and the benefits of drinking your fruits. I also learned how sticky frozen fruit gets when it remains on a dirty floor for too long.

I met a lot of cool coworkers. Some were also creatives, and on the path to something totally different. I found it refreshing to interact with humans that weren't doing the same thing I was. It gave me perspective and reminded me that life has so many roads for us to travel. I worked hard and stayed focused on my dancing.

Spiderman

You shot your web directly into my heart.
It grabbed the whole of it and marked a new start.
A web intertwined with compassion and care.
It hugged me softly and let me know you were there.
It had been a long while since I had felt anything like it.
I held on tight as we swung into a city brightly lit.
I was sure you'd never let go,
until that day came with a big blow.
It felt like I dropped hard onto the pavement below me.
It would be the first time I felt my heart couldn't see.
I fumbled on the street, all tangled in your web.
You ran off quick and left me for dead.
I tried to reason why my hero would do such a thing.
I had made my mistakes
and blamed me for everything.
The web was sticky, and thick.
It took me time to get untangled.
Even when I did, my heart was mangled.
It took me some good time to heal.
I guess my second big heartbreak was part of the deal.

P.S. - Spiderman

It was my first serious relationship after moving to LA. I was 23, and still figuring out a lot of things. I didn't know myself much at all yet, and with that came a lot of doubt and self-confidence issues. This person told me they loved me. They told me they wanted to stick it out with me. I was sure that this was divine timing, and that I had finally met the person that I would grow old with. A lot of people found their person around that age, so it didn't seem too far off. But I was a growing freelance artist trying to figure out how to navigate both my career, and an adult life. This person was kind, and I know they cared about me. But they were a bit lost themselves. We were about the same age, both trying to find what was the "right" thing to do in our early twenties.

We had both made mistakes, and the will to keep trying had faded. For a long while after the breakup I blamed them. I thought to myself "They didn't try hard enough." "They didn't love me enough." "How dare them start something they couldn't finish." But slowly as time went on, I realized it wasn't about any of those things. It was truly about the timing in our lives, and there were some lessons that both of us still needed to learn.

Years later this person emailed me thanking me for my friendship, both before and after the relationship. This felt nice. It was a small bit of closure. I was a good friend, and I did my best with what I knew at the time. And that was enough. If I could say one thing to my then-self, it would be "You are enough Nat."

The sun in my eyes

I had just washed my car,
and the sun was in my eyes.
Driving into the sunset there was nowhere to hide.
Suddenly two bright taillights,
took the next three seconds to the highest heights.
I slammed on the breaks, and tried to swerve,
but the reaction in my nerves
wasn't fast enough to serve.
My front left corner crashed into their back right.
I cringed at the crunching sound as I filled with fright.
Nothing left to do except accept this as the present.
I knew the most affected would be my monthly rent.
Thankfully no one was hurt.
My heart just began to invert.
Plunging down into a place I knew well,
knowing the repairs and insurance
would be anything but swell.

P.S. - The sun in my eyes

I had literally pulled out of the car wash just five minutes prior. The sun was low, and on its way to setting. It was right in my eyes, and suddenly the car in front of me slammed on its breaks. I tried to swerve to the right so as to avoid the impact, but I wasn't quick enough. Luckily there was an auto body shop nearby, and I was able to drive it just far enough to make it in.

The damage didn't look as severe as I later found out it was. I learned that day that there is a tank that sat in the front quadrant of my car. A tank that was expensive to replace. As it was a rear-ender I was found at fault. I understood. I should have been keeping a greater distance. But I hadn't, and I didn't have the money to repair it.

The car was deemed totaled by the insurance, and I had to say my goodbye. That night I sat at home thinking why the sun would do me like that?

"Why didn't I keep more distance?"

"Why was the sun directly in my eyes at that exact moment?"

This is when that stroke of bad car luck began. Shortly after this was when I got my bike and began my 3-year journey on two wheels.

Every Day I'm Hustlin'

There was one specific morning
when the alarm went off too early.
It was time for another day of work,
but my eyes were still blurry.
I was in no mood to ride my two-wheeled ride.
My body was tired, I couldn't lie.
When I finally stepped out,
the drops began to hit my face.
Great. Guess I'll have to pick up the pace.
My body exhausted,
not defrosted from the cozy sleep I wished to stay in.
But I lifted my chin, and made those gears spin.
Listening to the rain and my now rhythmic breath,
my muscles poked, as my jeans slowly soaked.
A familiar tune came to mind,
and its timing was divine.
"Every day I'm hustlin'" I said in between cycles.
This short pep talk was in that moment vital.
I sang it the rest of the way.
It really changed the start of that day.

P.S. - Every Day I'm Hustlin'

The mornings were early, and I was working two part-time jobs at the time. One in the mornings and another in the evenings. So, on the mornings when I had closed at my other job it was even harder to get myself up. And then, it doesn't rain too often in California, but you bet on this particular morning it was coming down heavy.

At first, I remember just wanting to cry the whole ride there. (Maybe I did a little.) But then I had this rush of a reminder that I was working my ass off for what I really wanted in this life. It hadn't always been a joy ride, but I was doing it, and I wasn't going to give up now.

I'm so glad that song came to my mind. I remember as I was singing the raindrops were hitting my teeth. But those words gave me just the push both figuratively and metaphorically that I needed that day. The reminder that I had come this far, and I wanted to keep going.

Truly, a day I'll never forget.

To the guy friends

I dedicate this to all the guy friends.
Ones that took what they needed and left the ends.
Ones that cared in the moment,
but not when that moment passed.
Ones that I put first,
and somehow, I ended up last.
I would offer a comfort more precious than gold.
Expecting it back was a story I told.
One I told myself to assure I would be loved.
That one day I would find my magic beloved.
Truly sad to see some of the friendships go.
Happy knowing new seeds would sough,
both for them and for me.
The only way forward is with love to see.
See that maybe it wasn't meant for forever,
but to guide us in the direction of a brand-new endeavor.
Thanks guys, for helping me along the wild path.
It all makes sense now.
I did the math.

P.S. - To the guy friends

This poem was written in a bit of rage, at a time when I hadn't found my person yet. This was my way of expressing exhaustion for all the times I gave so much of me without reciprocation. I couldn't understand. I would hear people speak of friendships turning into love all the time. I felt this was going to be the way I found my life partner. I wanted to fall for someone that made me feel safe before all the hard relationship stuff came into play. I wanted someone to laugh with and have inside jokes with. I wanted someone who understood my crazy profession and supported me through it.

Let's say that I had a lot of expectations on how I was going to find that person. Looking back, I realize maybe a few too many expectations. I had it all figured out in my mind, but what I didn't realize is that the universe had other plans for me. I had a hard time accepting this through my twenties. I wanted things to be the way I pictured them.

Along the way there were friends who became more than that, and in the end remained friends (for a while.) There was also some that made me laugh, as well as understanding my profession and supporting me through it. None of them ended up being the one I was looking and longing for, but I learned so much along the journey.

Despite the young frustration, I slowly evolved emotionally while understanding that all the experiences helped me know better what I wanted. I truly am grateful to everyone I deeply connected with. I learned so much from all of you. Each one of you helped me understand the things I did and didn't want in a partner.

So, Thank You.

Chapters

I don't only want to be called when you need me.
I want you to call because you're thinking of me.
Wondering where I am, or how I've been,
remembering moments that brought us zen.
But you stopped calling a while ago.
Now workdays are at our friendships core.
I thought we'd read more chapters together,
but your eyes got tired,
and you put down the book wherever.
I still keep the book dust-free on my shelf.
Grateful for our time, and the growth in myself.
It's been tough to find trust in new connections of life.
I'm seeing the value in being under appreciated.
When they walk away, it leads you back to you.
You are the one to face, with pace and grace.
You've been there all along.
Don't let anyone numb your song.

P.S. - Chapters

This one kind of goes with the last one. Thinking that I would read more chapters in my story with some people. But this one also goes beyond the romantic/physical aspect. Friendships also faded, and I closed the book on so many different eras of my life along the way.

Sometimes we believe we know how the story will go, but most of the time it takes us completely by surprise. Also, stories that we never thought we'd read come into our lives unexpectedly and are often a very pleasant surprise.

I like the analogy of each relationship/experience in my life having their own book on my shelf. Writing this book has been a portal for me to re-read some of those books and pick out parts that I can celebrate and be grateful for. Peacefully piecing together all the lessons that I've learned through the years.

I picture this big bookshelf sitting in the back of my torso, holding both the dear and dreadful memories of my life thus far. I'm proud of my book collection, and I felt compelled to share. Share because I know there are others out there with similar bookshelves full of books. Maybe this project will inspire you to re-read some of those books and highlight what the lesson was that you maybe couldn't see in that moment.

Happy re-reading.

The Switch

I didn't know the switch was there,
or what would turn it on.
It blind sighted me
with feelings of luck I'd struck upon.
An opportunity to leave the country,
teaching students oh-so hungry.
Taking their chances on an up-and-coming name.
I longed to venture with enthusiastic claim.
The only thing stopping me was my job at the shop.
Leaving weeks at a time would guarantee me the chop.
I was scared to take the leap,
but I craved separation from the herd of sheep.
I knew wanting more came with a risk.
I needed to act quite brisk.
After deciding to take that jump,
I could sense getting over a hump.
A hump of caution that kept me in the safe zone.
Now flying past fears and feeling more grown.

P.S. - The Switch

The year was now 2010. I was working part time at the juice spot and had picked up another part-time at a small mom + pops coffee spot. That, plus dancing, and not many bigger dance jobs in between, I was exhausted. I was wearing thin.

Then one day a friend that was visiting from Peru told me that she had an opportunity for me to teach some students at a school in Lima. I would get to teach and mentor for three whole weeks. I couldn't believe it! This was my ticket out of this city, and a goodbye to both jobs that I felt truly done with. I barely hesitated. I knew I wanted more, and teaching had always been a passion of mine.

This was such a beautiful experience for me. The students were so ready to learn and excited. It was so incredibly rewarding, and I got to see another corner of the world. I'll never forget it or the people I met there.

Checks

And as some things evolved,
the journey turned into quite a ball.
At times the patience was painful,
but the outcomes simply wonderful.
More checks on the bucket list.
Each one with tiny, exciting twists.
First time working for my biggest mentor.
An experience that personally opened a new door.
There I learned to embrace my divine feminine,
feeling into carrying myself with grand eminence.
It was a small group with a quirky vibe.
A comfortable feeling like that of a tiny tribe.
We traveled around for about twenty-four weeks,
with one famous brother we laughed with hurting cheeks.
They were times I'll never forget.
This moment in time changed my whole mindset.

P.S. - Checks

It felt like I turned on a switch after I made that decision to leave everything and just go. Something in my mindset shifted and the universe heard me. Jobs that I really wanted and wasn't sure I'd ever get started showing up. I was on a cloud in my own little world.

There was this feeling that I was really going to be able to do this consistently. Not to mention the fun I was able to have when I started to travel around more often. I started getting hired to portray more feminine characters as well. That was something new for me, but something I was ready to explore.

Of course, there were still times when my patience would be tested, but I had a new belief in what I was doing, and I could see where I was being appreciated as an artist. That felt extra good. I started checking off places I wanted to visit and was also making checks doing what I loved. It was a very exciting, and at the same time relieving time in my life.

The Pak

I was gifted a magical invite,
to join a Pak filled with mighty might.
They were eclectic and vivacious.
Their message and moves bodacious.
Highlighting individuality,
and embracing the you that is you.
A loving family that brought me somewhere new.
A tv land that wanted to showcase our creations.
Together we pushed through
expectations and fluctuations.
But together was the key.
Not one Fanny left behind.
We combined our superpowers,
while inspiring humankind.
Heroes in heels.
Warriors of peace.
Coloring the world through every single piece.
Now the most important part was the bond that formed.
It grabbed a part of my heart, and a light transformed.
I knew on their love I could always fall back.
My forever Fanny family.
The beloved Fanny Pak.

P.S. - The Pak

This poem is about my time on America's Best Dance Crew with Fanny Pak. This fun-loving bunch also came at the perfect time. A group of beautiful artists that I had known for years, would soon become a family forever.

Being on TV was hard. The producers were always looking for some conflict within the group. They wanted to capture us having a hard time. What was making things hard for us that week was a regular question.
Did they really want to see us win?

The praise would only come after we made it to the next round, and then the cycle would begin again. At times, it was hard. We had to produce new work each week. The turnover was insane. We were a group of nine artists trying to come together as one unified artistic voice.

But I wouldn't have wanted to have that experience with anyone else. The love that grew and the forever bonds that formed were the greatest gift. We handled every task with individuality and character. We were and still are a one-of-a-kind Pak.

Love you, Fanny Guwres!

A Month "Home"

My tank was empty,
and so was my bank account.
I needed time to recharge,
and a new game plan to surmount.
My motivation was low,
and my anxieties real high.
I needed new means of income to come by.
I envisioned staying 'home'
where my comforts could roam.
Where stability would hug me,
and responsibilities I could flee.
I could save some money on rent,
but I could feel this wouldn't be much of an ascent.
I could feel it in my gut.
I just needed to pull myself out of this rut.
But how to do so when you're already so low?
I focused on planting new seeds,
and watering them to grow.
It wouldn't be the fastest process.
But I knew day by day would come bits of progress.

P.S. - A Month "Home"

This point in my story is pivotal.

This was one of those times I let doubt take over. I had just done the show with The Pak, and contrary to popular belief the income for a contestant on a show like that is surprisingly low. My bank account was hurting, and I wasn't sure how I would continue living in LA. My previous roommate had "broken up" with me. Not really but she had a partner at the time, and they wanted to live together, and so I was without an apartment.

So, after the show I went home to Seattle. Going back to Seattle with little to no funds had me feeling like a failure. I wasn't sure that I could go back to LA even if I wanted to. I had lived in LA for close to eight years at this point, and I felt that I may have overstayed my welcome. I had done some amazing things and was proud of them.

There was a dance studio back home that I would teach at often. It was owned by the family of a High School friend of mine. I figured that some day when I was "done" with LA, I would retreat to that familiar space and teach there full-time. I always knew that was a possibility. So naturally I thought to myself, "It's time." Time to hang up the LA shoes and begin a new but familiar journey.

But here's the pivot. Something inside me told me "Not yet." I didn't know what that thing was, but I now know that was my intuition screaming "NOT YET!"

...to be continued on the next pages.

Bob's

Back to LaLa Land I went,
determined, recharged and content.
I needed a new way to make a living,
while I waited through some dream-come-true building.
I knew that I wasn't ready to give up,
and so, I leaned towards a familiar hot cup.
A cup of good coffee that is.
Techniques I was proficient in.
I already knew the biz.
I met a man named Bob
who dreamt of having his own shop.
I was confident that I could help him really make it pop.
I was back in a place I never wanted to be,
but it felt awesome to watch it all grow like a tree.
Connecting with customers,
and suggesting my favorite drinks.
Excited to have my own someday,
I dreamt of it in-between blinks.

P.S. - Bob's

Quite hesitantly, I decided to go back to LA after a month of being home. I was questioning the decision, and myself. I wasn't sure how I was going to do it all, but I knew that I had to try one more time. So, I started looking for a part-time job to help support me, again. (Insert eye roll emoji) I knew there was one thing I was good at, and I was sure that my resume would reflect that. Coffee.

I found a part-time barista job. A man named Bob was just about to open a coffee shop near one of the dance studios in a very popular area not far from where I was living at the time. He said he needed someone with coffee experience to help him get it off the ground and running. And so began my return to coffee and a new way of life that I wasn't sure I was ready for.

I found a friend who let me stay with her while I figured out my living situation. I was grateful to say the least. I slept on an air mattress in her living room that I would blow up every night and take down every morning so we could have a living room in her smaller one-bedroom apartment.

I felt like everything was working in reverse order.
"I should be more established by now."
"I should have saved more of my money."
I should have, could have, would have if... my inner critic was raging.

I didn't know how I had let myself get there, or why I was choosing to put myself through it all again. But I did know I wanted to give it one last fair shot, and I was going to do everything I could to make it a damn good shot.

Manifesting

I wasn't sure where I was going,
but there was this subconscious knowing.
There was more life to see,
even bigger and better than I could dream.
So, I started to really see it all with my mind's eye.
That eye had no reason to lie.
I made physical visuals I could see every day,
and ones that would repeat in my sleep state.
It took some real time,
but eventually they started coming true.
Gratitude was my attitude,
and it was finally shining through.

P.S. - Manifesting

My at-the-time roommate and I got along quite well. I kept thinking to myself how perfect it would be if we could just find an affordable two-bedroom apartment for the both of us. Of course, moving into an apartment gets very pricey when there is a deposit and 1st months' rent involved. I wasn't sure if I could make that happen at that time.

The Universe thought differently and spoke to me loudly when an apartment with two bedrooms opened in the same building that we were already in. The landlord agreed to a low deposit as we were already tenants and made it possible for us to take over very quickly.

It was truly heaven sent. I couldn't have asked for a better scenario. When the barista job lined up, I felt supported by the universe, but when this apartment magically appeared, I heard it in my gut very closely.

I could feel things were happening. I started a very consistent gratitude practice with a gratitude journal and created a new vision board in my new room. I had artists that I wanted to work for on there. I had countries I had never seen on there. I had a wedding ring and magazine clippings of the words 'power couple' right above it.

More on this to come...

Bobby

One rainy night home from rehearsal I came,
and stumbled upon a cute kitty so tame.
He meowed and meowed
like he was trying to tell me something.
I wanted to understand him.
My heart was thumping.
My roommate had a cat, so I shared a couple treats.
He gladly ate them,
and took off back into the streets.
Then the next night I came home
at about the same time.
He was waiting for me,
and a second snack time.
Then the next night the same,
but this time when I opened the door he darted inside.
He ran straight to my bed and laid on his side.
No collar or chip to find him his home.
I put up signs in the neighborhood
in case he had roamed.
The next day a woman called
saying he was a local stray,
and while she had fed him,
if I could afford it, he should stay.
So that's how Bob found me,
and lit up my whole life.
So grateful for his love.
He minimizes strife.
If you know him, you know,
he's a special kind of cat.
A bit more like a dog sometimes,
but truly a lover of Nat.

P.S. - Bobby

This is the story of how my cat Bobby found me. He has brought so much joy to mine and many others lives in his now twelve years of life. He is gentle and often cuddly. He's met a dog or two and lived in multiple homes.

When he found me, I had just recently moved into that 2-bedroom apartment. My roommate also had a cat. He was the type of cat who had a different mood every day. The day that Bob ran into the apartment, it was as if he knew, but he ran straight into MY bedroom. My roommate and her cat were already sleeping. I quickly closed the door to think about what my next move was. That first night he slept close to me the whole night.

The next day I took a picture of him and made signs to post around the neighborhood. We lived in an area with lots of homes, and since he wasn't too skinny or too dirty, I assumed he lived close. Then I got a call from a neighbor saying that she had been feeding him, but that he was a stray cat. She suggested I give him a home if that was possible for me.

And that was that.

Later, when work picked up and I was traveling a lot, Bob stayed long term with some friends of mine. They fell in love with him too. The love story continues, as Bob and I would someday relocate to Berlin, Germany where he would acquire a German cat brother named Bruce.

A standard drive

Sometimes a sput, kick or pow!
would send me on my way.
Getting into first gear was humbling every day.
I got a thirty-minute crash course
before I bought this car.
I truly believed I would learn not to stall.
Through many honks, and angry Angelinos,
I sent apologetic waves through my rear-view mirror.
She was an old and spunky red hatchback.
She gave me my freedom back,
and kept me on track.

P.S. - A standard drive

Now with the new job and the new apartment, I needed a car. I hadn't had one for about six months. I was asking friends for rides or taking the transport in between. Until one day, a friend said she was quickly setting off to college. She had been accepted to her dream school and was leaving in just a month or so. She wanted to sell her car and heard that I was looking for one.

Mind you, this was at the beginning of January in 2013. I had just recently secured the new living situation, new job and now a car... wow. Only thing was that it was a stick shift, and I had never learned to drive one before. So, before the sale, she gave me the quickest 45-min crash course in a parking lot.

That's it. That's all I got. What a ride, literally. At times, I was on a bucking bronco. Other times, I was stalled with angry people honking behind me. But with time we found a flow. That little red 1996 Honda Civic became a dear friend of mine.

But not for long... What I didn't know was that this specific car was highly favored in the street racing world. There were people out there hunting my car for parts. And those people found it. They found my car and stole it right off my street. The police found it two days later, two blocks from my home, completely stripped for parts. The ride didn't last long but I learned a lot in the process.

On to the Next

There was a dance class that I took.
It took me to a place I didn't yet believe I could hook.
I was in a hungry state,
this time the dance floor was my plate.
This time I wanted to show myself differently.
Some sharper edges, and ears open intently.
You can see it in the video,
I was laser focused.
Gliding softly,
like a feather light locust.
I remember the feeling so vividly,
confident, and connected melodically.
I had no idea who would later see this at a glance.
A glance that would bring me my greatest dance.
It's true, you never know who's watching.
Far away dreams now in my heart lodging.

P.S. - On to the Next

There is absolutely NO WAY that I could have thought or known, that the video footage from that class would be seen by a very important person, and later lead to my dream job coming true.

You just never know how things will turn out. You never know if your dream job is right around the corner.

Here are a few words I want to leave you with:

Always give your best, whatever that means on that day.
Believe in yourself.
Keep going.
Stay hungry.
Work hard.
Take care of yourself.
Mind and body.
You got this.
And on to the next.

The First Call

The first call was short,
it didn't last long.
I was booked for a secret project.
The shoot day hit me like a gong.
It was all a dream come true.
I spent the whole evening observing him and the crew.
In awe of the precision and work ethic.
From the back of the theater, I whispered
"This is truly epic."
I knew immediately
that I wanted to keep this feeling going.
Inspired to work hard and keep on growing.
While admiring the glowing and flowing,
a sense of knowing flooded me.
These are the people I want to surround myself with,
even when it feels gutsy.

P.S. - The First Call

I remember getting the first call and my agent said that it was a secret project with a top-secret name. I only knew that I would be shooting a music video, and that it was just a one-day job. I didn't find out until I got there that this music video would be for my dream artist. I didn't need to learn any choreography, I just needed to act as a party go-er in a beautiful theater setting. I wore a flapper type 1920's dress and was instructed to have a good time. Oh, and I sure did.

I remember feeling so elated, but also in a bit of a fog. Was this real? Was I really on set with one of my favorite artists. I watched him work awe struck. He had a hand in everything. He would consult with the band, then the dancers and choreographer, and finally the director to make sure the shot was perfect. I was trying to play it so cool. I didn't let my excitement take over. I just studied the scene repeatedly.

And what a magical scene it was. An old historic theater with red and gold accents. Everyone was dressed to the nines. The gentlemen were in suit and tie. It was a dream come true unfolding right before my eyes.

The Second Call

I was helping a friend with some visual work,
And when I checked my phone,
up curled a smirk.
I had missed a call that I needed to return.
The subject of the email made my insides burn.
The good kind of burn,
like when adrenaline floods you.
It felt like endless butterflies.
Excited to hear this news.
I gathered my breath responding calm and direct.
As soon as I hung up,
a shocked shriek was the after effect.
I re-assembled myself
before entering back into the room.
Everything felt in super zoom.
My heartbeat distracting.
My smile expanding.
Back to work I went,
entering a new reality with gracious intent.

P.S. - The Second Call

When I got the second call just a little over a month later, I just couldn't believe it. Get this... I originally missed the call from my agent. I was filming a project for a friend and was not near my phone when the call came through. When I checked my phone on a break I saw the missed call, and just below that was an email. The email's subject read: "!"

I quickly read the first sentence of the email, "Checking your availability to fly to NY on Monday to perform with your dream artist on not one, but two very famous late night television shows." Ok, it actually said more details but that's basically how I read it in my head. Holy! ... (insert all the words that you can imagine might follow.) I asked my friend if I could take a short moment to return a call from my agent.

I remember the studio that we were filming at and its industrial feel. Concrete everywhere, and not much color to be found. But I was lit from within with every color you can think of. I raced through the noisy hall to make the call just outside the doors where it was quiet. The conversation was short. My agent asked if I had read the email.

I said, "Yes! I am absolutely available."

He said, "Ok great I will keep you posted on flight details."

As I hung up the phone, I remember literally screeching out loud with joy and doing a herkie in the air. As I walked back to the room, my insides were hot. My smile felt like it would never come down. I took some deep breaths to calm myself down and went back to work. How? I'm not sure.

Time to suit up

One happy week later,
it was time to suit up.
The culmination of hard work,
and a very full cup.
I couldn't imagine what it would be like,
but in my heart, I knew it was time.
Moments of doubt flooded me often,
but I was ready for the climb.
The call had come in, and I needed to answer.
I had all the tools to finally be a professional dancer.
Ready to work with a team I deeply respected.
I worked hard to give my best version perfected.
I remember the day like it was yesterday,
a suit and a tie with an emotional array.
Not only would I do it,
but in front of millions.
An entertaining display of class, and brilliance.
It started and ended in a sweet flash.
After a few deep breaths my heart and mind had a crash.
The good kind again.
It felt like a splash.
Deep in my chest,
a kind of love whiplash.

P.S. - Time to suit up

A whole week passed between the call and when I would fly to the job. The longest week of my life. In the dance/entertainment world things can change in an instant, and I was fingers and toes crossed that I would get to do this job. Some part of me still couldn't believe it.

Eventually, I flew to New York, and we rehearsed for about a week before the first show. I got to formally meet the man that I had waited my whole life to work for. He was kind, funny and hard working. We were set to only perform one song. That felt simple compared to other jobs I had done. But this ONE song was so special. This one performance would live in my heart, and in television history forever. I could barely wrap my head around it, but it was time. It was happening and I tried to soak in every second with the deepest gratitude. I kept thinking, "This may be the only time I get to work with him," and if that was the case, I could die a happy Nat.

When it was finally showtime, the mood was set. We were all in suit n tie and I felt so dapper. No overly sexualized feminine outfit for this one. I felt home. One funny detail I remember is that the shoes they had for me were a half-size too big. The stylist told me that she would get me the right size for the day of the show. On that day, just hours before the show, she told me she was unable to get them. She handed me an extra pair of socks with her apologies. I had a short moment of panic, praying that the shoe size wouldn't affect my performance. Thankfully it didn't.

It was truly one of the most amazing weeks of my life. I will never forget it.

The First World Tour

Around the world I went.
Time away from home I spent.
From pillow to pillow at each different hotel,
often feeling like a queen being treated so well.
The screaming fans at the show each night,
kept my adrenaline pumping simply at the sight.
Strangers that became family,
while learning about each other affably.
We'd find each other's smiles amongst the nightly roars.
A group filled with overflowing passion at the core.
The team for the task, that's just what it was.
Acknowledged daily by gracious applause.
The traveling was always the hardest part,
but that disappears when you remember
this was a wish from the heart.
At times it felt like life was standing still.
Getting back to it leaves no time to chill.
You sometimes sacrifice relationships and special events.
The show must go on regardless of current contents.
But you wouldn't trade one second for the world,
knowing you've lived out your own epic dreamworld.

P.S. - The First World Tour

Good news: I did get to dance with that artist again.

Many more times in fact. After those first initial shows, I was brought on for a round of promotional tour in many different places. Each show was a bit of a one-off, and the schedule varied dramatically. I was riding the wave. The cloud for that matter. Nothing could bring me down.

Then one day when we were in rehearsals, the choreographer came in and said he needed to talk to us about something. He continued to say that if we accepted, that we were being asked to go on a world tour starting in just a couple of months. Holy! (Insert all the words you can think of that would follow.)

A WORLD TOUR!
MY FIRST WORLD TOUR!!
I was 28 years old at the time.

Almost 10 years after moving to LA to pursue this big dream. There were times where I honestly wasn't sure if I would see this day. But here it was. My stomach sunk and my smile grew. I thanked the choreographer for his trust in me and hugged all the dancers in pure excitement. I had no idea what this adventure entailed, but I was ready to find out.

That First Big Show

It felt like electric currents running through my veins.
Nerves in my muscles, a relief I couldn't gain.
The music started booming, as we all took our first place.
Preparing ourselves for this remarkable race.
A race that we knew we could run.
One that was also full of fun.
I just had to take those first few steps.
The crowd was roaring, I felt I couldn't misstep.
I took a double deep breath before loading in.
I was anxiously ready to win.
Win the race of my dream come true.
Excited to conquer this journey new.

P.S. - That First Big Show

In the beginning, it was all a blur. Rehearsals were fun and productive. But that first big show was a feeling I'll never forget. The adrenaline that coursed through me felt like lightning bolts of joy. The roar of the crowd was one I had never heard before. That deafening roar is what would power me through those first few steps.

I would start the show in a lift that would raise up from underneath the stage. I remember a huge smile branding my face as soon as I looked out into the crowd of people screaming.

The in-ear monitors we wore were something I needed to adjust to. Later, when I got adjusted, I would often sneak one out just to hear that crazy roar all over again.

Oh yea, and dancing in a full custom suit also felt pretty frickin' cool.

Highs & Lows

As I said before,
life doesn't stop.
It keeps moving through the highest highs,
and the lowest drops.
I saw the drop up close and personal.
No matter the dream, it was not merciful.
It showed me that the people I love are real,
and might also need my support while they heal.
It wasn't easy feeling my brain and heart divided.
My heart craved to ride the waves,
while my brain provided.
For my family I would do anything.
Seeing them in pain caused a great sting.
I strived to be the light amongst the darkness.
I vowed to be their hearts harness.
The best news is,
we all surfaced above these deep waters.
Each one with a new perspective,
and sharpened honors.

P.S. - Highs & Lows

There was so much to be excited about. Tour was and still is one of the coolest and craziest things I've ever experienced. All the preparation was the buildup into those first few shows. Then came finding a flow as a tour family both on and off stage. It was a 360° experience that kept me learning and growing the whole time. I was truly floating on a cloud. Until I was quickly brought back down to earth by real life things.

My mom fell quite ill just a month or so after the tour had started. I felt so conflicted. I wanted to be home with her and my family, but I was living the biggest dream of my life at the same time. I took most of my tour breaks at home in Seattle, while helping financially when I couldn't be there physically.

Two opposites happening simultaneously. I guess that's life for you. Thankfully, my mom was able to see the show live in my hometown. What she experienced that year gave her a second shot at life and at how she wanted to live it.

Although it was so difficult, I am grateful that she is healthier now because of it. I guess tour was also placed in my life as a bit of a healthy distraction, as well as a financial support from something that may have otherwise taken me down. Those are the kind of moments when I'm reminded that every season has its reason.

Matriarch

A powerful leader,
very loved by their tribe.
An incredibly dependable woman.
A feeling only few can describe.
She relies on herself for the goods that she needs.
She plants the seeds and plucks all the weeds.
She's always ready for the task at hand,
plotting a plan for a crash land.
Just in case she gets exhausted while giving it her all,
she'll take a deep breath to crawl and stand tall.
Again and again, she knows just what to do.
Her emotional survival tactics
always carry her through.

P.S. - Matriarch

This word encompasses how I felt in that very conflicting time. I felt responsible to make sure that everyone was ok. That everything was going to be alright. Even when I didn't know if everything would be alright.

I put on my big girl pants and tried to not let my family see how scared I really was. I became the emotional matriarch of sorts. It wasn't an easy role to take on, but I understand now that I was in that position at that specific time because I was ready for it.

I was able to exercise my emotional strength, and in the process of celebrating my wins, it was also a reminder that life comes in waves. It's never all great, and it's never all bad. There is space for both in every instance of life.

Postpartum

It was as if I had birthed a baby.
One that had grown in my heart a little more daily.
For years I anticipated the arrival of this dream,
imagining it even in my sleep stream.
At times, it felt I may not see it,
but deep down I knew I couldn't quit.
Then one day it arrived in a package of surprise.
I spent the next chunk of time creating emotional ties.
Then one day that dream came to an end.
The end of an era, and time to ascend.
But it didn't feel much like lifting.
It felt a little closer to sinking.
Sinking away from the light I had built up so bright.
The next logical move further and further out of sight.
My insides fought with might.
My mind gave up the fight.
For a while, it felt like a piece of me was missing.
I longed for more of this incredible feeling.
Dropped back off in a world I once knew,
now just a space unfamiliar and blue.
It took me some time to get out of that head space,
and back into a new groove with pace and grace.

P.S. - Postpartum

We did 128 shows.
26 countries.
14 months on and off the road.

We closed the show in Las Vegas while also recording a film adaptation of the show. That next day, I was on a flight back to reality. I wasn't so sure what that meant anymore. I had given up my apartment before the tour started. I had put most of my important belongings in a storage unit that I shared with a friend.

That meant I had no apartment to come "home" to. Things in the city had changed. New buildings had gone up, others had shut down. Life kept gong while I was away, and I felt like a foreigner in my own city. I had to push onward, even when I felt this deep hole in my gut.

I missed my tour family.
I missed traveling.
I missed my job, the stage, the joy.
I was sad.

A new kind of sad, one I had never felt before. I had given birth to this baby of a dream come true, and now it was gone from one day to the next.

First Space

I always dreamt of having my own space,
with calming feels in a serene, and simple place.
The headquarters where I could plot my next move.
Some close corners to receive my every groove.
Then one day it appeared,
at a moment when my head was clear.
It was a chance I couldn't pass up.
I had worked so hard to fill up my own cup.
And there I was,
getting the keys to my first place.
A little nervous but taking it all with pace.
Feeling accomplished, and excited.
My dreams and goals finally united.
A space to grow, and it felt enchanted.
Extremely grateful for where I had landed.

P.S. - First Space

At this point I had to wipe my tears, put my big girl pants on once again, and start looking for a new place to live. The coolest part was, by not having an apartment while I was touring, I was able to save up a good chunk of my earnings. I had a budget that I wanted to stay in, and I knew that I wanted to live alone for the first time in my life. This had been on my bucket list since I had first moved to LA.

I turned to craigslist. (Is that still a thing?) I found a few places and planned to see them in person. I saw 2 or 3 places before I looked at one that I felt was closest to the place of my dreams. The rent was just a little bit out of my budget, and when I tried to talk the landlord down, he said he couldn't go any lower.

I got back in my new car that I had recently purchased, (another bucket list goal I got to check off,) and sadly drove away from what I believed was not the dream place after all. Ten minutes later, the landlord called me back and said he was willing to make the drop in price. He said he wanted me to have the place, and so became my first one-bedroom apartment.

I couldn't believe it. I signed the lease just a couple weeks after returning from tour. I was back on a cloud. A different one this time, but nonetheless a cloud of my own that I was so proud of.

It Lingered

It lingered for way too long.
I guess I wasn't their favorite kind of song.
Or so it seemed,
when their eyes no longer gleamed.
They had heavy things on their heart.
Things that were slowly tearing them apart.
They pulled at me from every seam,
even when I thought their intentions I could see.
My edges hardened and burnt to a crisp.
Their toxicity brushed through me like a thick mist.
Maybe they'll never know how much that time hurt me,
or maybe it weighed on them just as heavy.
Glad that we're both free
from the pressures that it brought,
both learning new things
that back then we wouldn't have caught.

P.S. - It Lingered

This one was hard for me to write. I spent too long holding on to someone who didn't love me the way I deserved. I was convinced that this person would change. That if I was good enough to them, or made the right efforts, that then they would want to do better. I learned the hard way that those things were not true.

The right person who loves you will show it to you just the way you are. I held on to the idea of what it 'could be' for far too long. Maybe someday it could have been just as I imagined it, but putting myself down and compromising my mental wellbeing in the process was never the answer.

• IMPORTANT POINT: This person was not a bad person.

Still aren't. They were simply at a point in their life that wouldn't allow them to heal from their own traumas, and therefore projected them onto their relationships. Just as they may have witnessed as a child.

One of my favorite quotes is: "People can only meet you where they have met themselves." This speaks volumes when you are in a relationship with someone romantic or not. You may not be able to see eye to eye because you both probably have things you need to work on, but you may not be able to work on them together. Nurturing your mental health is and should always be your first priority.

Thirty

Many asked me how I was feeling,
as the day grew nearer.
Like something would magically pop up
to make it clearer.
I got it.
I was turning thirty, but I wasn't so scared.
A sign that the twenties were leaving,
and a fresh start prepared.
I wanted to see something I'd never seen.
Magic for my eyes, a beautiful new scene.
Thirty called for a solo soul-searching trip.
Forever images I'd keep in my mind's memory chip.
So, I made plans to stay with a very nice couple.
They treated me as a friend
and showed me their favorite corners.
Whether out on the water, or enjoying great food,
it was everything I needed for an expanded mood.
It was my first time visiting this incredible place.
And from my twenties I felt I could unlace.
There was more life to embrace.
New feelings to face.
Hawaii, you were an unforgettable moment in time.
Our exchange was impactful
and reset me for another climb.

P.S. - Thirty

Thirty was transformative for me.

I didn't feel this mid-life crisis feeling. (That came later :) I was at a point in my life where I felt on top of my own world. I felt like there was nothing I couldn't do. I had achieved some of my greatest goals, and it felt like I was just getting started. I was ready to keep going.

My twenties were hard. They pulled me down in ways I couldn't imagine. They also taught me so much about how I wanted to continue forward. It was my first big caterpillar into butterfly moment.

My first big confidence boost as an adult. My first time living and traveling alone. I bought my first car all on my own. I felt really grown up. I was ready and so excited.

Hawaii was a beautiful start to that new chapter.

Underwater

It was on the actual day of my birth.
The ocean displayed nature's incredible worth.
I couldn't wait to plunge in.
Longing to feel a cleanse from within.
The water was warm and crisp,
I felt it kiss my toe tips.
I dove in excited,
and was immediately met with a feeling frightened.
As I came up for air,
another wave crashed into my head.
Sending me tumbling into the oceans bed.
I didn't know up from down,
there was no air to be found.
The current grabbed a hold of my heart and my ring.
It would now be the oceans, or so it seemed.
When I finally found the air,
I couldn't believe I was still there.
I guess thirty was meant to wake me up,
and remind me to keep filling my cup.

P.S. - Underwater

On the day of my 30th birthday, I met up with some friends that lived in Hawaii. We all decided to go to a beach and lounge around for the day. The water looked so inviting. I could feel myself drawn to it. What I didn't know, was that this beach was specifically known for its strong undertow. Just seconds after I had taken my first dip, I started walking back to the shore and BOOM! It felt like the wave had punched the back of my head, and I went back underwater, this time un-willingly.

I tumbled around down there for what felt like minutes but was just a few seconds. I had never felt this feeling be-fore. I of course panicked first. I thought "oh wow, I might just die on my 30th birthday." But then I had a moment where I thought to myself, "you can't resist the waves, you have to just let go." Immediately after that I felt one of my rings slip off my finger and seconds later I was above the water again. As I hurried back to shore this time, I looked back knowing that the ocean had taken my ring with it.

Let's say this wasn't just any ring. It was a ring that I had bought myself in the first week after I had moved to LA. I never took it off. It was a silver horseshoe, which when I bought it, I thought would bring me some good luck. As I sat safely with my friends back on the beach, I started to really contemplate what had just happened. My friend said, "I guess you left a part of you with the island." That hit me hard. This small ring that had symbolized my journey in LA thus far was now with the island of Hawaii almost exactly ten years after I had moved to LA.

I thought about how so many of those dreams that I felt I needed luck for, had already come true. How much of this dream life that I had set out to accomplish was happening right before my eyes. I was also grateful to be alive.

Accepting Flow

I started to realize
I was missing a small element.
A tiny shift that would bring a relief so decadent.
I was resisting the flow
of things as they came.
Slowly seeing things
in a different frame.
Allowing things to be as they were,
not how I wished them to be.
Inviting in the present
began to set me free.
Learning to release the worries of past or future,
kept my brain waves flowing simple and smoother.
It wasn't easy at first,
sometimes my brain in my heart submersed.
I couldn't always think straight,
but deep breaths always brought me a clean slate.

P.S. - Accepting Flow

That first year that I lived alone, was the first time that I took my yoga and meditation practices seriously. It was the first time I had the uninterrupted space and time to do so. This was a game changer. I had always enjoyed the peace that filled me from a yoga class but doing it alone in my own space brought with it a new peace.

I could hear my own breath and go at my own pace. I could move in the ways that felt right for me on that day. This brought about so many feelings. I realized how much I had been resisting. I had this perspective on how things would/should unfold in my life. And this, kept me from accepting things as they were. It would stop me from breathing through the moments that felt tough. I would grip and eventually slip along the path that was laid out for me wishing another path would unfold before me.

But slowly this feeling subsided. I was able to breathe through and accept more of what was in front of me. This allowed so many more doors to open. The next few years would bring opportunities I never thought I would have. I was reminded that ultimately, I'm not in control. That everything happens as it will, and it's best to just let them flow.

Letting Go

And in those same relieving breaths,
my parasympathetic system found some rest.
But there was another step to be made.
One that sometimes made me afraid.
Afraid because change meant discomfort.
I felt enough of that I had suffered.
It takes time to find things and people that feel right.
Things that make the magic in your heart bright.
And then to think... let go of those things?
Hoping somehow, I'll find new wings.
But who knows where I'll land?
I want to be prepared.
Somehow blinded by the past,
I become visually impaired.
More concerned about what I've done wrong,
than accepting no answer and moving right along.
I have to say, it's gotten a bit easier.
But it can take its time like a burning meteor.
In the meantime, I'll gaze up at the open sky,
knowing it's all in the stars to clarify.

P.S. - Letting Go

This is a poem about exactly what that surrender felt like. It's not easy to let go of the things or people you love, even if they may not be able to love you back the same way. The surrendering is part of your healing. It's the part where you accept that there is nothing more to do. That your focus must shift toward something new.

Maybe a project that you have been meaning to start or continue working on. Maybe prioritizing yourself, and your wellbeing. Your choices will vary based on where you are in your mind and heart. But we must give ourselves the grace of surrender.

"Pain is inevitable, but suffering is a choice."

To allow things to be as they are, and not force them into what we think they should be. To be mindfully aware and actively stay in the present moment is called a practice for a reason. It will not always be easy, and it will never be clear overnight. With even a small amount of attention each day, then we practice focusing on the feelings that feel better, rather than the worry, shame and negative loop over something we cannot change.

Teaching Sparks

Teaching sparks my heart,
even when it doesn't feel lit.
Even when life has me pushing through with grit.
I could be exhausted as I walk in,
and leave energized to the max.
With eyes on me I want to deliver the facts.
Facts of my experiences,
both in dancer and human world.
I deliver them with joy,
passionately furled.
Knowing that my encouragements can stick
just as much as my corrections.
Reminding them dance is fun
is one of my biggest intentions.
I count out with cadenced rhythm.
Often sing out in a not-so euphonious algorithm.
A map to the feelings felt and sounds heard
is what I deliver.
Then as the music turns on their ears pleasantly shiver.
It is one of my greatest joys.
It brings me perpetual poise.

P.S. - Teaching Sparks

I started teaching dance at age 16. That was now over 20 years ago. At first, it was a job that I found to be quite fun, and easy to do. It wasn't an office job, and I was thankful for that. In the beginning, it was something that I knew I could do well, and that would help make me some extra cash. But over the years, it flourished into something much grander. Something much more purposeful.

I realized that in every dance class I stepped into, there was a group of people excited to share this love for dance with me. They were looking for a good time along with some guidance on how to navigate this extremely physical, and often emotional journey.

After I started working professionally, my gratitude for the teachers I had growing up grew tremendously. I understood how imperative their hard work and dedication was to my development as an artist. I understood that they weren't just teachers. They were my guides. They gave me guidance not only in movement, but in how to navigate the world through dance. There was discipline and repetition. There was fun and expression.

The realization that I am now able to offer that same guidance to my students, fills me up with joy and purpose. I will teach dance until I can't anymore. I am so thrilled to have already been and continue to be a part of so many other dancers' journeys along the way.

Here, a quick thank you to those who have and continue to put their trust in me as their guide. I truly never take it for granted.

Inspiration Station

It was a trip I had planned for,
but I hadn't planned for what was to come.
A stroke of inspiration from a group I had just met.
I told them about an idea,
they said, "why haven't you done it yet?"
That was the question I needed
to launch me into a new mindset.
Why hadn't I started?
I got to work right away.
It would take me another year and a half
to finally display.
And even then, it just wasn't the right time.
It was just the beginning of a new artistic climb.
Something fresh,
a territory uncharted.
Something emotionally whole-hearted had started.
I felt rejuvenated, and ready to start up again.
Eternally grateful for those two gentlemen.

P.S. - Inspiration Station

It was 2016, and I was still coming down from my first tour postpartum. I was longing for a spark of inspiration. I wasn't sure what would be next after realizing one of my biggest dreams. How could I top that?

I wanted something new and exciting, so I took a trip to Germany to visit some friends and do some teaching around the country. I am so grateful to have made connections in LA with some awesome humans who lived overseas and were willing to help me organize some work on the other side of the pond. I took this trip with the sole intention of enjoying myself and exchanging dance with students and friends. One night after a nice dinner we all got to chatting about "what was next for me?" I dreaded this question as I felt I had absolutely no idea.

But I blurted out, "Someday I want to write a book. A book about my story and how it has all unfolded thus far."

One of them casually said to me "Well, have you started?"

"No, I haven't." I replied. "I wouldn't have the slightest idea where to start."

He said to me, "You just have to start."

In that moment, I felt the light bulb illuminate just above my head. My heart started racing, and adrenaline pumped through my veins. I would start writing a book! That was my next new and exciting project. As soon as I got back, I began writing a long form book about my story. I was intimidated and unsure of how to go about it, but I wrote 43,500 words about me and my life. Those words are bound in a 3-ring binder here on my bookshelf at home. So many parts of that book were inspiration for this one.

The Lump

I was randomly just feeling around.
I wasn't expecting to uncover this ground.
A surprisingly solid lump.
The touch of it made my heart jump.
Thoughts raced through my confused mind,
wondering what the scan would then find.
For a couple weeks I wondered in worry,
hoping the results would come in a hurry.
Every possibility met me in those weeks,
emotions soaring to the highest peaks.
Thankfully, the results came back uneventful,
and with myself I became even more gentle.
This body so precious of mine.
Always working for me while I'm on the grind.
Grand gratitude flooded me deeply,
with some new priorities in order neatly.

P.S. - The Lump

I found a lump in my breast.
I think I was putting lotion on, and there it was. As you can imagine all the emotions flooded me. Those are the moments where you feel so completely out of control. Lost to be honest. It puts into perspective how quickly things can change, and that although at times we feel healthy and invincible, the body is not.

Our bodies are an extremely complex structure that work for us every second of every day, and sometimes we don't take care of it the way we should. And even when we do, things can develop regardless.

I saw a doctor shortly after and had my first mammogram. Of course, it took a while (which felt like forever) to get the results back. This was the most agonizing part. I didn't want to share any news with my family and friends until I knew for sure what it was or wasn't. I wandered about my life in worry while trying to stay positive.

I remember lying in bed every night, and while taking deep breaths I would try to visualize this lump dissolving. I am fortunate to say the scan showed that it was a benign cyst and the doctor told me I had nothing to worry about but to keep an eye on it and get regular exams. It was a big scare, and my new perspective was a huge launching pad to stay more aware of my body. To give it the care it needs while checking in more often.

Sprinkles of work

There were sprinkles of work
that kept the momentum going.
The breaks in-between
are what kept my heart flowing.
I wasn't stressed about much.
The sprinkles showed up as such.
I was in a new stage.
Turning over a new page.
Uncovering things I didn't even know I wanted to do.
Everyday really did feel brand new.
It was an era of simply feeling.
Showing up each day was the healing.

P.S. - Sprinkles of work

Amidst the focus I had on writing my book, I believe this encouraged some surrender around my dance work. I had saved a good chunk of money from tour, and I was able to relax into the things that I wanted. Doing the things I really wanted, allowed me to open new doors in my heart. I was being called to do jobs that I never even knew I wanted to do.

I started working with more choreographers that I had never worked with before. This felt like a coasting era. I felt like I was surfing the work wave that had started when I booked that first big tour. I was feeling recognized for my talents and had the freedom to choose which jobs I wanted or didn't want to do.

It was a tremendously liberating time. The jobs were sprinkled about. They didn't come all at once, but I understand looking back now, that that period was a direct result of me feeling ease and trust in myself as an artist and a human.

A patient of patience

There're always good days and bad.
Waiting calmly while time plays its hand.
Lately, restlessly anticipating,
while staying gentle in creating.

Internally turning.
Awaiting my next big rush.
Hanging onto little sparks
from the last creative crush.

Itching for my next dose of serotonin.
Now more than ever,
a vital component.

Reliving times that once relieved this dis-ease.
Every
last
drop
I want to squeeze.

My blood, sweat, and tears
have carried me here.
Capsules of love.
Triumphant treatments for fear.

In the process of craving,
I find more and more healing.
Ushered into new chapters,
I invite more and more feeling.

Finding patience in being a patient
to my own creative addictions.
Not feeding them too often.
Sticking to my aspiring convictions.

P.S. - A patient of patience

This was almost the title of this book.

Having patience with anything can sometimes be one of the hardest things to endure. When you are waiting for something exciting. When you are sad and want that feeling to pass. When you are unsure of where life will take you next. When you doubt yourself along the way.

Patience is at the core of most of our lives. Having the patience to see where things go and try to "go with the flow" can also be maddening. This poem evolved from the roller-coaster of emotions that I've felt while navigating so many aspects of my life. My career would have never been what it is now, if it weren't for my patience and persistence to keep going. To go back to that coffee shop just before that dream job came. My partner came to me later in life than I thought he would. Even when I was met with people who couldn't love me the way I loved them. I had to have the patience and trust that whoever my person was, they were on the way.

In a way, I often felt like a patient of my own patience. At times, it hurt and at others it showed me exactly why it didn't work out any sooner. It's by no means an easy practice, but I promise it's worth it.

Round 2

This one caught me by surprise,
just as much as the first.
I found out in a parking lot.
Waited to get in the car for my outburst.
After the first, I wasn't sure
if I'd ever get another chance.
All I knew was that I wanted another dance.
To represent this incredible artist once again.
With new fire, and more knowledge than back then.
So off I went,
on a second trip around the world.
With a group of familiar faces,
my confidence whirled.
The excitement oozed from me daily.
Happy notes spilled from an uplifting ukulele.
My rose-colored glasses were on.
From my worries I was withdrawn.
It was time to venture into the woods,
while basking in the sunlit goods.

P.S. - Round 2

It's true, I found out in a parking lot on a chilly November evening. I found out that I was being asked to go on a second world tour with my dream artist. I, a friend, and our mentor standing just beside his car.

He said "So, do you wanna go on tour again?"

I remember my hands dropping in between my legs as I hunched over to catch my breath. I don't remember the exact words that came out next, but I think it was something along the lines of "ABSOLUTELY!" This was followed by an excited giggle, and shriek as I had expressed the first time. This time in good company, we all smiled at each other while doing a little victory dance in that parking lot.

I really couldn't believe it but was ready to get to work. We would start again just one month later. I had another job to do in the meantime. This job would be the first time that I was assisting a choreographer on a big award show. Some serious dreams come true at the end of that 2017.

I was ready for a Round 2, embracing all the things I had learned in Round 1. I had fresh eyes and was excited to approach the whole experience a bit differently this time.

A Bowl that was Super

This big memory
was connected to another big one.
I was working two jobs at once.
We prepared for a couple months.
It felt both easeful, and exciting.
A brand-new chapter was under bright lighting.
An incredible team for an impressive task.
There really wasn't anything more that I could ask.
For I felt my place in that space,
I wouldn't leave one second to waste.
I could breathe in the excellence,
while feeling the energetic resonance.
I felt more than in my element.
I led with a flow so eloquent.
I cried happy tears in the middle of the whole thing.
Still not quite able to believe in a second spring.
Springing into that next chapter with grace,
with every moment that got me there to embrace.

P.S. - A Bowl that was Super

I was told that we would start rehearsing for the tour, but at the same time we would begin developing the structure for what would be one of the biggest performances of my life.

That show that happens at the half of the biggest yearly football game. Holy sh*t! One of the most watched events of the year. It's estimated that 103 million people tuned in that year. That is absolutely the largest audience I have ever performed for.

We had a large group of dancers for the performance, and each one of them has been a part of my dance journey in some way. It was a family affair, and the whole process leading up to it felt just like that. It was hard work, but also plenty of laughs and good times. A few weeks with friends that I will never forget.

We performed in Minneapolis, Minnesota and in our set was a tribute to an incredible artist who had recently passed the year before. I remember that we weren't dancing during the tribute, so I was able to watch it from my position for the next song.

On that special day, I remember being moved to tears on the field. In awe of the life, I was given, but also the life I dreamt up and worked so hard for. A whole journey had brought me there, and a whole new one was ahead of me.

No Great End

There's no great way to end this story.
As the stories keep magically unfolding.
But I hope these here bring you hope and a smile.
One that will last you even just a little while.
I feel stories are meant to be shared,
even when we may be a little scared.
I believe it unlocks doors in my heart,
and hopefully yours too.
To heal the collective,
we must stay connected.
Both through art,
and through heart.
We can plunge into life's waters together,
supporting each other through the now and forever.

P.S. - No Great End

The poem says most of it, but I will elaborate just a bit. It's been so hard for me to choose where this book will "end." Of course, it's not really an end as my story keeps unfolding. But the reason I chose to write this book in the first place, was to share my stories and connect with you all in a new way.

For years, dancing was the expression that allowed me to connect to others. Now I'm ready to connect in a new way and express other sides of my artistry. Expressing through another artform that I find so impactful.

I hope my story inspires you to keep following your dreams. To keep expressing the things that make you, you. To allow in all the joy that this life has to offer you. The beautiful part is we don't know if when our life ends, if that's really the end. I like to believe it isn't. I like to believe that our souls live on in some way forever. My hope is that what we do here with our time on this Earth will impact the people we meet and those that journey with us, as well as future generations both now and possibly forever.

With Big Love,
-Nat Gilmore

© 2024 Natalie Gilmore
Publisher: BoD • Books on Demand GmbH, In
de Tarpen 42, 22848 Norderstedt
Print: Libri Plureos GmbH, Friedensallee 273,
22763 Hamburg
ISBN: 978-3-7597-3719-9